PUBLICITY STUNT!

GREAT STAGED EVENTS THAT MADE THE NEWS

CANDICE JACOBSON FUHRMAN

Chronicle Books ▲ San Francisco

Printed in the United States of America, Hong Kong and Japan

Library of Congress Cataloging in Publication Data
Fuhrman, Candice.
Publicity Stunt! / Candice Fuhrman.
p. cm.
Bibliography: p.
Includes index.
ISBN 0-87701-509-0
1. Publicity—History—20th century.
2. Public relations—United States—History—20th century. I. Title.
HM263.F84 1989
659—dc20
89-34368
CIP

Produced by Wink Books, Forest Knolls, California
Cover and book design: Charles Fuhrman Design
Executive producer: Theo Gund
Researcher: Patricia S. Moore
Copy editor: Suzanne Lipsett
Production and typography: Steve Wozenski
Proof reader: Candace Demaduke

WINK
BOOKS

Distributed in Canada by Raincoast Books
112 East Third Avenue, Vancouver, B.C. V5T 1C8

10 9 8 7 6 5 4 3 2 1

Chronicle Books
275 Fifth Street
San Francisco, California 94103

C O N T E N T S

A Charlie Chaplin lookalike contest held at the Liberty Theater in Bellingham, Washington, in 1921, attracted hundreds of participants. This publicity stunt, staged to promote the premiere of *The Idle Class*, was duplicated in theaters across America.

ACKNOWLEDGEMENTS

I am grateful to the many generous people who have gone out of their way to help me with this project— from the very beginning, when it was only an idea. First and foremost I must thank Theo Gund, my partner and benefactor, without whose support I could not have taken the time to work on this book.

The late Marty Weiser, one of the first people I interviewed, was an invaluable source of information. I feel privileged to have met him and real sorrow at his passing.

Whenever I said "publicity stunt," people would say "Jim Moran." I learned he had retired in Ajicjic, Mexico and flew down to interview him. It was a thrill to meet him and hear the details of his many great stunts first hand.

Among the many others who contributed sources and stories, I especially want to thank Jerry Carroll, Gary Carson, Ron Chan, Brett Decker, Henry Erlich, Cris Evatt, Jet Fore, Kim Freilich, Richard Geiger, Samuel Gill, Mary Ann Gilderbloom, Tony Habeeb, Jinx Hone, Ralph Novak, John Polanda, Violet Ray, Steve Rubenstein, Jonathan Schenker, Joey Skaggs, Mac St. Johns and Jane Wesman.

Special thanks go to David Barich of Chronicle Books, who acquired this book; researcher Patricia Moore, who went beyond what was asked and uncovered many great stories; copy editor Suzanne Lipsett, whose suggestions really improved the manuscript; and production editor Steve Wozenski, whose attention to detail was invaluable.

My daughter, Karie, is a joy and has been an enthusiastic reader and editor. And finally, to my husband Charles, who collaborated on this book from the beginning, traveling with me to interviews, helping to shape the concept, designing a beautiful book, and selecting the photographs, I dedicate this book. His love and affection have changed my life— my gratitude runs over.

Introduction

Once when I was a young child growing up in Los Angeles, I saw the Cinerama Theater turned into a gigantic Easter bonnet. I didn't know it then but that was a publicity stunt—on behalf of the movie *Mame*. Another time, on a streetcorner in Hollywood, I saw a man sitting inside an enormous bottle building a model ship. That too was a publicity stunt—an elaborate one to promote a now long-forgotten television quiz show.

And every Saturday I went to the movies in Hollywood, where the theaters were constantly staging contests and giveaways. Coming and going, I'd see costumed people performing, stopping traffic, and drawing crowds. I didn't realize it then but my formative years were being shaped in the publicity stunt capital of the world and these experiences would color my view of life forever.

A natural talent for exaggeration led me inexorably to a career in publicity. For ten years I headed my own public relations agency in the San Francisco Bay Area. My own personal best publicity stunt was an audition for cats to be in an upcoming cat calendar. More than a hundred cats showed up, along with reporters from the Associated Press, three local television stations and the Sunday *Examiner*. A close contender for my best was the backwards roller skating event I organized down San Francisco's famous Lombard Street ("the world's crookedest street") to publicize the forthcoming "Roller Disco Extravaganza."

But my efforts were modest compared with the best of the many thousands of stunts that are hatched by attention seekers every year. Part of the mix of information that appears daily in what is called the news, publicity stunts are created specifically to attract media coverage. They are usually conceived and prepared well in advance of execution—requiring weeks or even months of Machiavellian strategy sessions and reams of supporting printed materials and props.

A publicity stunt can be the brainchild of one individual with an axe to grind or a single component in the campaign of a highly paid public relations team. The intention in attracting media coverage can be highly commercial (to sell a client's product) or deeply idealistic (to protest an injustice). But whatever the impetus, spending the time and effort is always a calculated gamble, because there is never any guarantee that the media will cover the stunt.

Over the years many of my clients asked me to come up with ideas for publicity stunts. This was always easier said than done. How do you determine whether an idea will be so irresistible that it will become legitimate news? Why are some events scorned by the media while others make page one? I began looking for stories of successful stunts, to see what others had done.

My search led me first to Hollywood, where, in their heyday, the major studios maintained entire departments, called "exploitation departments," devoted to publicizing their stars and movies. It seems that the Golden Age of Hollywood, roughly thirty years from the early 1920s to the late 1940s, was also the golden age of publicity stunts. For every movie released, an entire campaign, sometimes years in the planning, was mounted to promote it. Special "press books," lavishly produced and illustrated, suggested hundreds of imaginative promotional ideas that theater owners could implement in their own towns. Each studio stationed field publicists in the major cities whose job it was to create advance publicity for incoming movies through publicity stunts, advertising, and community tie-ins.

But the techniques employed by Hollywood had an earlier genesis. The legendary P. T. Barnum, whose career spanned much of the nineteenth century, is often credited with originating the publicity stunt. He was certainly one of the first to use the media to promote his ventures. But I discovered that many great stunts had been executed before his time. In fact, no one really knows who "invented" the publicity stunt; the creation of an event to attract news is as old as news itself.

Finding examples of publicity stunts was a challenge in itself. I found very few direct references to publicity stunts in card catalogues and book indexes. Nowhere are "publicity stunts" collected and saved for posterity. No how-to books have ever been written. In gathering the stories in this book, I had to comb old newspapers and extrapolate stunts from the reported news. I also interviewed dozens of contemporary public relations professionals and journalists and followed up their leads.

As my collection of stories grew, I began to notice that some stunts could be grouped into distinct categories. Soon I had identified a number of stunt types that surfaced over and over again as seemingly surefire ways of attracting the media. Ultimately, I used these categories to organize this book. Still, I couldn't hope to cover all the stunts I turned up, or even all the best, in this informal roundup. Instead, I've picked the most imaginative, the most successful, and the ones so funny or outrageous to me I just couldn't pass them up.

In recent years, the publicity stunt has fallen on hard times. It has gained an undeserved, unsavory reputation that ignores the creativity and imagination a good stunt requires. Nowadays, most public relations people disown any connection with publicity stunts, referring grandiloquently to their more comprehensive role in creating a client's "total image." But the more stunts I uncovered, the more

I wanted to showcase the special genius behind them. And I also saw a chance to illuminate that shadowy area where news and stunt intermingle—an area that grows greater and murkier every day.

Publicity stuntsters have always shrouded their activities in great secrecy —comparable to the way magicians jealously guard their techniques. The assumption is that a public that is aware of the publicist's methods will not buy the product that is being promoted. The media, too, have a stake in secrecy by suppressing their reliance on publicists to bring them these tales. Although they use the term "publicity stunt" as a pejorative when referring to the crudest efforts, they are always hungry for colorful stories.

This book reveals to the general public the behind-the-scenes links between the media and the public relations profession. But, more than that, I hope it will restore the publicity stunt to its rightful place as a valuable tool in the publicity seeker's bag of tricks.

**The Cinerama
Theater in its
Easter bonnet**

Chapter 1

An Illustrated History of the Publicity Stunt

From Penny Newspapers to Global Communication

Wish-news is a type of publicity that nearly always breaks on the front page. It is news so thrilling, melodramatic, and heart-gripping that every city editor wishes it were true.

Harry Reichenbach

The original lithograph illustrating life on the moon, as reported by the *New York Sun* in 1835

Never let the facts get in the way of a good story.
An old wire service exhortation

Many early publicity stunts in the United States were outright hoaxes, especially those perpetrated in the late nineteenth and early twentieth centuries. That was a time when newspapers themselves engaged in hoaxes, sending reporters out to create stories. A rough-and-tumble frontier mentality prevailed, tall tales flourished, and larger-than-life robber barons ruled commerce. In a very short period, America changed from an agricultural to an industrial society and the population itself doubled. The traditional ways of exchanging information changed with the times.

In the beginning there was only print. Although newspapers flourished in America from colonial days on, the early papers had limited circulation. Edited and written for the privileged classes, they were sold by subscription only and intended for the well educated. It wasn't until the 1830s that the general population was large enough and literate enough to support mass-circulation newspapers. At that time, a number of penny newspapers were founded, the first papers to be affordable to the masses. One that gained great circulation was the *New York Sun*. Started in 1834 by printer Benjamin H. Day, it had twenty-seven thousand readers by 1837, five thousand more than its eleven New York rivals combined. The *Sun* was a lively paper featuring police reports and lots of gossipy short items about the society leaders of the day. Constantly on the lookout for ways to boost circulation, in 1835 the *Sun* perpetrated an astounding hoax that still ranks among the all-time greats.

The paper printed a series of articles that purported to describe life on the moon. Crediting these "discoveries" to a well-known astronomer of the day, the articles claimed that a telescope had been perfected that could reveal details of the moon's surface. Four-foot tall, winged creatures, with apelike facial features, were said to be cavorting across a lush landscape. Not surprisingly, the series created an international sensation. Newspapers all over the world reprinted selections from the articles while openly debating their veracity. The *Sun* reported the doubts of the other papers while continuing to insist on the accuracy of its stories. Meanwhile, the demand for back copies was so great the paper had to run its printing press an extra ten hours a day. And when the hoax was finally revealed, people didn't seem to mind. Although rival papers denounced the stunt, the *Sun* had achieved the largest circulation of any paper in the world up to that time.

Creating a story to build circulation became a common practice of the nineteenth-century newspapers. The *New York Herald* pulled off one of the most famous when it sent journalist Henry Morton Stanley to Africa in 1871 to search for the missionary-explorer Dr. David Livingston. Stanley took several years to find Livingston, but all along the way he sent back stories to the *Herald*. When found, Livingston was surprised to learn that he had been missing.

The *New York World* sent reporter Nellie Bly on a trip around the world to see if she could beat the record of Jules Vernes's fictional hero in *Around the World in 80 Days*. Bly filed her stories about her progress from exotic ports and considerably boosted the *World*'s circulation. And, incidentally, she beat the record by eight days.

But the real heyday of the penny press came in the last two decades of the nineteenth century. Joseph Pulitzer and William Randolph Hearst each owned New York City newspapers that battled for circulation through massive promotions, sensationalism, and journalistic exploits.

HEARST MAKES NEWS

You furnish the pictures, I'll furnish the war.
William Randolph Hearst

Probably the most infamous of the journalism stunts was perpetrated by Hearst in his *New York Journal*. His biographer said of him in *Citizen Hearst*, "In truth, Hearst was not a newsman at all in the conventional sense. He was an inventor, a producer, an arranger. The news that actually happened was too dull for him, and besides, it was also available to the other papers." Hearst has been accused of precipitating the Spanish-American War through a series of circulation-booster stunts.

In 1896, before the perfection of the technology to reproduce photographs in newspapers, Hearst sent artist Frederic Remington to Cuba to sketch "Spanish atrocities." After a few days Remington cabled Hearst: "Everything is quiet. There is no trouble here. There will be no war. I wish to return." Hearst cabled back, "Please remain. You furnish the pictures, I'll furnish the war."

Soon thereafter, a reporter was sent to break into a Cuban prison and release a Cuban girl incarcerated for conspiring against the Spanish government. Hearst employees actually bribed prison officials to ignore her escape, and a breakout was staged that was turned into sensational headlines for the *Journal*. Later the young woman toured America speaking out against Spain. Such incidents, combined with Hearst's inflammatory editorials, eventually led to Congress declaring war.

My dear sir, the bigger the humbug, the better the people will like it.
P. T. Barnum

The new penny papers were constantly on the lookout for the bizarre or notorious—anything to build circulation (on which advertising rates were based.) Naturally, they were a receptive audience to the colorful band of press agents and flimflam artists who trained with the carnivals, circuses, and vaudeville shows and followed the trail blazed by P.T. Barnum.

Phineus Taylor Barnum was one of the best-known people of the nineteenth century. And he was possibly the first to become famous not for what he did himself but for the way he promoted others. Some called him the "Shakespeare of advertising." Barnum's career spanned sixty years from the 1830s to 1891 when he died. His first real success, long before he began his famous circus, was a hoax.

In 1835 Barnum began exhibiting an old black slave named Joice Heth, who claimed to have been George Washington's nurse. This would have made her 161 years old. First Barnum rented a hall in New York City and mounted an extensive promotional campaign. Posters and ads told the story of the amazing old woman and included a bill of sale signed by George Washington's father. Heth told anecdotes about the young George and was apparently very convincing. The story was a sensation and was covered in the New York papers for weeks. Then Barnum took Heth on the road.

When attendance began to wane in each city, Barnum would write anonymous letters to the editor of the local newspaper. The letters would accuse Heth of being a fake. One letter said, "Joice Heth is not a human being at all. What purports to be a remarkably old woman is simply a curiously constructed automaton, made up of whalebone, India rubber and numberless springs ingeniously put together and made to move at the slightest touch according to the will of the operator. The exhibitor is a ventriloquist, and all the conversations apparently held with the old lady are purely imaginary."

The controversy resulted in a new spurt of attendance, just as Barnum had hoped. Throughout the rest of his career, Barnum was to resort to writing fake letters to the editor whenever he wanted to generate publicity. He would write letters signed with made-up names both denouncing himself as a humbug and defending himself. The ploy never failed to work for him, but it was just one in a repertory that he expanded upon throughout his colorful career.

Consider the crowd-pleasing Tom Thumb. He was an authentic midget, but that in itself wasn't enough for Barnum. When discovered, the diminutive child was five years old and living with his parents in Bridgeport, Connecticut. Recalling the old fairy tale about the mythical Tom Thumb, Barnum rechristened the youth. He then created an impressive lineage for him and added six years to his age. Barnum figured that people would be even more amazed by an exceptionally small eleven-year-old.

Changing names and creating a false background for a person became a tradition that entertainment press agents used routinely until recently. In the early days of motion pictures, the

Mrs. Tom Thumb
with borrowed
baby

biographies of the stars were almost always completely fabricated. Exotic backgrounds made better copy than the real thing.

Barnum rolled out all his advertising and publicity artillery to promote Tom Thumb. Almost immediately, the midget became internationally famous and one of Barnum's most profitable exhibits. And anytime interest in the tiny guy appeared to flag, Barnum would put his fertile imagination to work. The world thrilled to the announcement of the birth of Tom Thumb's first child. Lithographs of the "proud father" and his wife Lavinia with an infant in her arms were carried in newspapers everywhere. Shortly thereafter the borrowed baby was returned to its real parents. The Thumbs never did have any children but the publicity stunt had served its purpose—attendance at their appearances had increased substantially.

As the proprietor of a kind of "freaks" museum in New York City, Barnum was constantly on the lookout for unusual exhibits. In the mid-nineteeth century there were many exotic animals and deformities of nature that people had never seen before. Barnum changed his exhibits frequently and publicized them

vigorously. Once he exhibited a bearded lady named Madame Josephine Clofullia. She was a married woman with a luxuriant black beard whom Barnum had brought over from Switzerland. When the initial attendance was light, Barnum paid a man to file a complaint with the police accusing Clofullia of really being a man. Her subsequent arrest and acquittal made many headlines.

The related strategies of the engineered arrest and the trumped-up lawsuit, by the way, became favorite tools of many press agents in the years that followed. Today we see few faked arrests but an unusual lawsuit is still guaranteed to attract a lot of media coverage.

Barnum didn't start his legendary circus until the 1870s. At the time, many small circuses were traveling by horse and wagon across America. But Barnum's circus soon outstripped all others in attraction and scale. He was the first to move a circus by rail, and his spectacular advertising and publicity techniques preceded him wherever he went.

Early circus press agents would travel ahead of their shows and tack up handbills in taverns and stores. Sometimes they would stand in the town square, ring a bell until a crowd had gathered, and then regale their listeners with exaggerated descriptions of the coming attraction. Barnum's circus had a separate publicity and advertising department with its own railroad car. The advertising team would arrive in a town in three stages, in the first stage plastering posters on everything in sight. About

a week later the second contingent would arrive to poster anything left and meet with reporters to plant advance stories. Finally, the twenty-four-hour men would show up to make sure the newspapers had enough information, talk with top officials in the town, and check the parade route. The circus parade, which could be a lavish spectacle involving a cast of thousands, was the final ballyhoo that lured the crowd to the big top.

In early America, many communities banned circuses and other traveling entertainment on moral and religious grounds. The parade was used to give the community a free look at what was being offered and to demonstrate the innocence of the show. Parades became a reliable publicity vehicle to help promote an event or a concept, though nowadays it can be difficult to get a street permit, and most parades tend to be civic-

sponsored affairs commemorating historical events. But corporate sponsorship of a parade float is a modern device that public relations people still use to enhance their client's image. Macy's Thanksgiving Day parade is an example of a public relations idea that has become a national tradition.

The parade is the most elaborate version of "street bally" (short for *ballyhoo*) or the art of attracting a crowd. Barnum was a consummate artist of "street bally," generating endless schemes to start people talking about his attractions.

Barnum boasted openly about the many times he managed to fool the public through the media. He asserted that people benefited because illusion is a public need. "Every sham shows that there is a reality," he proclaimed. Barnum's strategy was to let people in on their own hoodwinking. He gloried in his many nicknames such as "Bamboozeleem" and "Humbug." "The titles of humbug and the prince of humbug were first applied to me by myself," Barnum wrote in his autobiography. His constant hoaxing and blatant manipulation of the press were hot topics in the newspapers of his day, both in America and Europe. Although many criticized him, few could resist his latest tale.

New press agents are being born every minute. You can hear forty or fifty of them howling or laughing on every city block.
Editor & Publisher, 1909

By 1900, telephone and telegraph wires connected the entire nation and daily newpapers numbered 2,326, with a total combined circulation of about fifteen million. National magazines with circulations of one hundred thousand or more were additional sources of news, and advertising had become the major source of revenue for both newspapers and magazines. Now large-scale commerce dominated the national scene and the captains of industry held to the principle "let the public be damned." This inspired a generation of muckrakers, who relentlessly attacked the business moguls in shrill denunciations that received wide coverage in the popular press.

The public relations profession was in its infancy, embodied mostly in the press agents who worked in entertainment. But as the muckrakers proliferated, business hired growing numbers of press agents to counter their attacks. When John D. Rockefeller refused to talk to reporters after a mining accident at his company in which many people were killed, he became one of the most hated men in the nation. But all that changed a few years later when he hired Ivy Lee, one of the first press agents to specialize in working for industry. By counseling Rockefeller to give away dimes wherever a crowd gathered (and a suitable number of reporters were there to record it), Lee is credited with completely transforming the Rockefeller image. The "giveaway" is a type of publicity stunt that continues to flourish to this day.

People in business began to understand the advantages of cooperating with the media and in fact using them to promote the business point of view. The first independent publicity firm, The Publicity Bureau, was founded in Boston in 1900 by three former newspapermen. Its success led to the formation of many other firms and to

John D. Rockefeller bestowing a famous dime on another lucky recipient

the addition of publicity departments to advertising agencies.

As they multiplied, the newspapers banded together in a professional organization, The American Newspaper Publishers Association (ANPA). Among its main purposes were policing advertisers and establishing guidelines for working with advertising agencies. Advertisers were now the newspapers' primary revenue source. But buying advertising space was expensive and more and more businesses were turning to press agents to get them a free mention in the editorial space. The cost of hiring a press agent was significantly less than hiring an advertising agency and paying for ad space. Furthermore, a news story about a business is considered more creditable than an ad. Heretofore many newspapers had the practice of "puffery"—giving editorial space to purchasers of advertising space, but now the ANPA sought to eliminate such practices.

The threat of revenue loss led the ANPA, in 1908, to declare war on the press agent. To *Editor & Publisher* magazine, L. B. Palmer, the general manager of the newspaper group, gave an account of the rather mild incident that precipitated the war:

> During September 1908, George Van Cleve, an advertising agent of this city showed me a half column write-up in the *Evening Telegram* about the Breslin Hotel, with a picture of a woman with a Merry Widow hat trying to enter the revolving door. About a stickful of the article was human interest, the balance, a description of the beauties of the hotel.

The inference was that the press agent for the Breslin Hotel had planted the woman in the revolving door, which undoubtedly he had. But the idea that such a publicity stunt was a revelation to anyone is extremely unlikely.

As its opening attack in the "war," the ANPA set up a "Free Publicity Department" to monitor the activities of press agents. Each newspaper was asked to report incidents of obvious publicity stunts or story planting so the others would be able to identify them. Then the association hired a private detective to "hunt down" the press agents responsible for the stories, wherever they might be. In 1909, the investigator reported that he had uncovered more than one thousand press agents operating in New York City alone.

The ANPA campaign against press agents eventually reached Congress. In 1913 a bill was introduced into the U.S. Senate that sought to make press agentry an offense punishable by a fine of from $50 to $1,000. The bill failed to pass, but it probably would have been unenforceable in any case, for by then the press agent was an indispensable member of the news-gathering team. Although their place has never been more than grudgingly acknowledged by journalists, even today a large percentage of the news that appears on any given day has been provided by press agents. As Louis Wiley, business manager of the *New York Times* put it way back in 1919, "It is a perfectly understandable thing in this complex, highly organized age that publicity representatives should perform a useful, legitimate function."

To be sure, while newspapers were debating their merits, business was hiring press agents in record numbers. By 1917 *Editor & Publisher* was reporting that "the press agent has come into nearly every business." In an article titled "HOW THE PRESS AGENT PUTS IT OVER PAPERS," Joe Jackson, a reporter, noted, "Press agenting in its swaddling clothes was a crude business compared to its present state of development. City editors would laugh merrily today at some of the most famous stories that the romancers of the past 'put over.'"

Actually, Jackson was wrong. The most outrageous publicity stunts still lay ahead. The movies' domination of the entertainment industry and the emergence of the studio system would turn the publicity stunt into a veritable industry.

On July 19, 1920, a story appeared in the *New York Times* headlined "DRAG LAKE FOR WOMAN." It reported that police had spent several hours dragging the large lake in Central Park near 73rd Street for the body of a woman believed to have drowned. Earlier, a lady's purse and hat had been found beside the lake, and suicide was feared. Inside the purse was a hotel key and a slip of paper on which a woman's name was written.

The story continued the next day. After a thorough search, no body had been found in the lake. The management at the hotel said that the missing woman was a Japanese actress who had last been seen the evening before. As the investigation continued, it became clear that the story had been staged to interest the public in an upcoming movie in which the actress was starring.

The story sparked outrage throughout the city, and it seemed that a press agent had finally gone too far. Editorials denounced the hoax and the New York City district attorney, Edward Swann, began investigating the possibility of prosecuting press agents who attempted to deceive the police or newspapers with false reports.

"SWANN TO RUN DOWN PUBLICITY FAKERS," screamed the *New York Times* on July 26, 1920. "It strikes me that the person guilty of this hoax is guilty of disorderly conduct at least. His conduct would certainly cause the policemen who were fooled to desire to club him," said District Attorney Swann. Referring to a law just passed by the New York state legislature that made it a misdemeanor to furnish a "false and untrue statement of fact to a newspaper with the purpose of having it published," Swann announced his determination to collect evidence to prosecute.

It didn't take long for the investigators to turn up the hand of Harry Reichenbach, whose schemes on behalf of his theatrical and motion picture clients had already made him a legend.

THE REICHENBACH TOUCH

Everywhere people clamoured to be fooled and it was gratifying to see how much they appreciated it when they were well fooled.

Harry Reichenbach

The background of Harry Reichenbach, regarded by many as the founder of modern motion picture publicity, was a press agent's dream. At the age of thirteen, he actually ran away from home and joined the circus. By the time he was seventeen he had twice traveled around the world with a magician known as the Great Reynard. When he arrived in New York to introduce Reynard to the "big time," he brought with him a mastery of the promotional principles that he had learned in the carnival world. These he applied first to Broadway entertainments and then to motion pictures. As he tells it in his autobiography, *Phantom Fame:*

By the third day I was a thoroughbred New Yorker. By the fifth day I had planted my initial publicity stunt to let the mammoth town know Reynard the Great had arrived. It was a simple backwoods recipe composed of a lost jewel, a fire and the heroic rescue of a young girl, but the mighty cosmopolitan press lapped it up.

Soon after his arrival in New York, Reichenbach witnessed the dramatic rescue of a little girl by a fireman, and decided to use that event for his own purposes. Secretly he arranged with the fireman to deliver one of Reynard's rings to the lost and found department of a newspaper and to report that he had been aided in the rescue by a mysterious hero. The newspaper naturally ran the story describing the ring, and when the owner came forward to claim it, he was none other than Reichenbach's client, the Great Reynard. Needless to say, the magician launched his act to a surge of public interest.

When Reynard left New York to continue his tour, Reichenbach stayed behind. After working as a press agent for various Broadway producers for a number of years, he was hired by the fledgling motion picture industry. By the midteens, movies had completely captivated the nation. Hollywood was becoming the production capital of the business, and the studio system was evolving. Still, it was difficult in those early days to gain critical recognition for the new medium. Reichenbach remembers:

> Before 1916, it was impossible to get more than a line or two into the papers about a feature picture or its star. In that year when *The Hypocrites* opened at the Longacre Theatre I attempted to persuade the press through advertising to review the picture as if it were a play. The editors put on a sneer of scorn that almost disfigured their faces permanently.

With that kind of reception from the newspapers, a publicist really had to be creative to crack the news. And Reichenbach was more than equal to the task.

One of his most elaborate publicity stunts took almost as much advance planning and rehearsal as the movie it promoted. The story began when an Arabian sheik and his retainers arrived in New York and held a press conference. They had come all the way from Turkey, they said, in search of a beautiful virgin princess believed to have eloped from Stamboul with an American. She had been betrothed to a Turkish prince, they said, and had left behind a fortune of $100 million. The case had everything: royalty, millions, romance, mystery, and seduction—the perfect recipe for terrific publicity.

The initial press conference was packed with reporters, and they covered the search in daily updates. The newsreels—Fox's *News Weekly, Kinto,* and *Pathe Weekly*—paid the sheik to pose in Central Park. Every aspect of his wardrobe and habits was reported in breathless detail. A few days later new headlines blared that the missing virgin had been found. And within a week a new movie *The Virgin of Stamboul* opened in New York. The film told the story of a wealthy Turkish princess abducted and taken to America. Its producers had feared that the trite plot would fail to earn back the movie's investment. They had hired Reichenbach to do what he could.

Reichenbach had spent weeks planning this stunt. The royal retinue actually consisted of eight unemployed Turks he had found in New York's Little Turkey. Reichenbach had had the group trained in royal comportment by a former diplomat crony of his and dressed in authentic splendor by a theatrical costumer. The designated sheik had been drilled in his lines for over a week. Even the august *New York Times* fell for the scheme, running the inital story with a four-tiered headline:

SHEIK HERE SEEKS
$100,000,000 GIRL

Fiancee of Amir of the Hedjaz
in an Arabian Nights Elopement
with an American

WORLD WIDE SEARCH
BEGUN

Father, "the Rockefeller of
Turkey," Dies of Grief after the
Disappearance from
Constantinople

The Virgin of Stamboul, a rather tortured melodrama with little fresh to recommend it, scored a new record at the box office.

Later that same year, Reichenbach pulled off another stunt, one that would become a classic. Producer Samuel Goldwyn approached him to publicize *The Return of Tarzan*, the third in a series of Tarzan movies that seemed destined to oblivion. Reichenbach was a natural for the job, since in his youth as a press agent for the circus, he had come to understand the eternal news value of an exotic animal. For *The Return of Tarzan* he conceived a stunt that combined that old chestnut with a couple of customized news-getting strategies.

Eight days before the movie was scheduled to appear, a man checked into the Hotel Belleclaire in New York City and signed the name Thomas R. Zann in the register. With him he brought a huge box containing, he said, a piano. He asked that the box be hoisted into his room. The next day Zann called room service and ordered a delivery of fifteen pounds of raw red meat. The curious management went to the room and discovered a full-grown lion in residence. The police were summoned and the reporters soon followed. The *New York Times* ran the story on the front page: "PET LION AGITATES HOTEL." Ads promoting the lion's appearance at the movie premiere linked Mr. Thomas— "T. R."—Zann with the forthcoming movie.

NOTICE

Mr. T. R. Zann, the daring adventurer who took his pet
L I O N
into the Belleclaire Hotel
will appear personally
N E X T   S U N D A Y
in conjunction with the new
FILM STARTLER

**T H E   R E T U R N
O F   T A R Z A N**

at B. S. Moss' Broadway Theatre
Broadway at 41st St.

Reichenbach's *The Return of Tarzan* stunt was what I call a "shaggy dog" stunt, in that it required an elaborate buildup and story to unfold with no seeming connection to the client's product until the "punchline."

Coming in the same year, Reichenbach's two stunts made him a likely suspect in District Attorney Swann's investigation. On July 27, 1920, Swann sent him the following letter:

Dear Sir:

Complaint has been made to this office, that you, under an alias, framed an alleged suicide charge, knowing the same to be false, with the intent to create publicity, by which false report and manufactured situation you caused the police to consume two days time and labor in searching for a person that you knew was not missing.

If the facts in this charge against you are correct, it is a violation of the criminal law. If the facts contained in the charge are not correct, I write in order to give you an opportunity to correct them in any respect in which they are erroneous.

I must ask you to call at this office on Friday, July 30, at 12 o'clock.

There is no evidence that Reichenbach planned the district attorney's attack, although it might well have fallen into the "arrest" category of publicity stunts. But whether planned that way or not, before it was resolved the case had attracted nationwide attention and even involved the White House. The *New York Times* account on July 30, 1920 gives such an amusing and detailed account of Reichenbach's manipulations that I reprint it here in full.

TUMULTY LETTER IN PRESS AGENT INQUIRY

IT TOLD HARRY REICHENBACH FAKE MEXICAN RAID WOULD BE TAKEN UP WITH PRESIDENT

CALLS SUICIDE HOAX CRUDE

Publicity Man Cites Plan to "Kidnap" Clara Kimbell Young as Sample of His Work

District Attorney Swann, who has been investigating the part played by press agents in the "suicide" in a Central Park lake of a fictitious character in a Japanese film play, began to make inquiries also concerning quack publicity methods in connection with a series of motion picture plays, including "The Virgin of Stamboul," a "Tarzan" picture and a film described briefly as "The Cannibals."

Mr. Swann questioned Harry Reichenbach, a press agent, who denied implication in the suicide fake, which he denounced as "crude." He admitted, however, that he was the creator of the missing Virgin of Stamboul affair and the Belleclaire lion episode and that he was now engaged in using his wits to promote a film play dealing with cannibals.

At the request of Mr. Swann, Reichenbach produced contracts calling for the payment of $1,000 and $1,500 a week for his services, which were described as "exploiting, publicizing and attracting attention to "The Virgin of Stamboul" and "Creating sensational manifestations" in connection with it. Another contract showed that, after the Belleclaire lion episode, the film concern had inserted a clause which placed on the press agent the responsibility for damage to animals, property or person that might arise from the "sensational manifestations."

Got Assurances from President

When offering evidence that the Japanese fake was not in his own style at all, Mr. Reichenbach instanced as a typical conception of his own the plan of having Clara Kimball Young kidnapped by Mexicans and held for heavy ransom until rescued by eight blond cavalry men.

"I went abroad for the Creel Bureau doing exactly this same type of work," he said. "I spent $8,800 of my own money and got shot up with shrapnel. I could not get the money back and so I tried to get it back in trade. I got the assurance that President Wilson would back me in this little bandit raid. Clara Kimball Young did not even know it was going to happen."

Mr. Reichenbach took from his pocket a letter on White House stationery, signed by J.P. Tumulty, who said that the matter would "be taken up." The publicity man said that the "matter" referred to was the proposed Clara Kimball Young border episode. He was unfortunately interrupted before he explained why the idyllic little international embroilment was canceled.

"I went through Italy doing press agent work for President Wilson," he said, "I made them bow down and pray to him before they did to the saints, and I spent my own money doing it. I deserved some return."

Where he Got "Publicizing"

The publicity man said he was ready to make oath that the first he had ever heard of the Japanese suicide was on Tuesday in Pittsburgh, when he saw a reference to it on the bulletin board of *The Pittsburgh Dispatch.*

When the Reichenbach contracts were being read Mr. Swann interupted to ask:

"That word, 'publicizing,' where did you get that?"

"President Wilson used it at a dinner before he sent us abroad, and he used it in his final instructions before we sailed," replied Reichenbach.

Mr. Reichenbach told Mr. Swann that his tricks and devices were only a variation of usual publicity methods. He instanced pictures of Mrs. Cox making biscuits which have appeared since the nomination of Governor Cox; Governor Coolidge pitching hay and other pleasing pictures of candidates as speciments of publicity not differing from his own work.

"I see," said Mr. Swann, "It's the same old thing, dumb-show and noise 'to split the ears of the groundlings.' I believe that is classical, Mr. Cox," addressing a Shakespearian scholar who happened to be in the room.

"I'll make a note of that." said Reichenbach, taking out a pencil. "I'll have to remember that."

Sees no Harm in a Good Fake

Mr. Swann declined to say whether he thought Reichenbach was innocent.

"I agree with the newspapers and the District Attorney in resenting this clumsy Japanese suicide fake," said Reichenbach after leaving the District Attorney's office, "but I can't see what harm a good fake does to anybody. I used to be a newspaper reporter, and I was the worst newspaper reporter that ever lived. Then I was an advance man, getting $75 a week. In the last six years at the line of work I am in I have made $300,000. I gave my ideas away for twenty years before I found I could sell them.

"I was the man who had May Yohe missing seven years ago or so. They dragged the lake and they dragged the Hudson, and the next day we opened at Hammerstein's. I planted that story up in New England where the big picture of the matinee idol was stolen from the lobby of a theatre and then found in a young ladies boarding school. As for this law against slipping misinformation to newspapers, what is the matter with going over to New Jersey and doing it?"

Mr. Swann said that he would question several other press agents today in the hope of discovering the perpetrator of the Japanese suicide fake.

Facsimile from the

New York Times,

July 30, 1920

In this way Reichenbach used Swann's investigation as a soap box for virtues of the publicity stunt. Ultimately, Swann decided not to prosecute anyone but the stories did have an effect on the future of press agentry. The open season on press agents, begun with the ANPA's attacks in 1908, was starting to offend many of the new practitioners.

Chafing at the notoriety, they sought to distance themselves from their circus-trained forefathers. In a strategy perfectly appropriate to the profession, they declared a name change. Henceforth, the press agent would be called the public relations director.

This new title was the brainchild of a man often called the father of public relations, Edward Bernays, a nephew of Sigmund Freud. In 1920 Bernays was testifying in a trial involving his former client Enrico Caruso. When asked his occupation, he answered, "Counselor on public relations." The next morning the *New York World*'s headline proclaimed, "FIND NEW PROFESSION IN CARUSO SUIT TRIAL."

Bernays spent much of his career trying to "upgrade" the press agent's image. He taught the first class on public relations in 1923 at New York University, and in that same year *public relations* was listed as a category in the yellow pages. Gradually, the profession of public relations began to diverge from its entertainment roots, but throughout the twenties, often called the Age of Ballyhoo, it was the flamboyant attention-getting strategies that set the tone.

BUSINESS TAKES OFF: THE TWENTIES

If there is no excitement ready-made, some must be manufactured.

Silas Bent, *Ballyhoo*

The 1920s were the madcap era of flagpole sitting, goldfish swallowing, and marathons of all kinds. Prohibition spawned an entire underground industry—and every nightclub and speakeasy that sprang up had to have its own press agent. Services were offered on a freelance basis from $1 an hour to $100 a day. In their book

Shipwreck Kelly made a career of flagpole sitting. Here Roth Motor Cars benefits from his media appeal.

Showbiz, Abel Green and Joe Laurie, Jr. recalled this nutty time:

> Showmen had a choice of music on trucks, parachute jumpers, stilt walkers, fat men, clowns, captive balloons, walking dolls propelled ahead of autos, mechanical animals and horses, mechanical men, blindfolded car-drivers, rube impersonations, men-who-never-smile, auto trucks built like zeppelins, human blimps and flying humans.

Into the fray jumped a brand-new medium, radio, the next link in the global communications industry. At first radio itself was primarily a publicity vehicle. Entertainers would go on the air for free to talk about their upcoming shows. But soon radio became a bona fide entertainment medium itself, creating its own pantheon of stars. As with television later, entertainment executives worried—justifiably—that radio would draw the audience, and receipts, away from other media, and the greater their anxiety the heavier was their reliance on the public relations experts. In 1926, radio weighed in as a contender when NBC debuted its national programming in a spectacular event staged at the Waldorf-Astoria and attended by more than a thousand reporters and celebrities. Soon advertisers were sponsoring programs and radio stars were developing their own box office draw. By the end of the decade, radio was the nation's fourth major industry, with an estimated fifty million listeners.

Meanwhile, the nation was being swept by fads, many of them planted by the proliferating "public relations people." Edward Bernays was hired by a major tobacco company to think

of a way to encourage American women to smoke. Heretofore, it had been considered unladylike for women to smoke in public. Bernays's brainstorm was to hire a number of prominent debutantes to march in New York's fabled Easter Parade defiantly smoking. Their pictures, carried by wire services nationwide, changed the smoking habits of American women forever.

By the way, Bernays, who continued his penchant for naming and renaming, called this publicity stunt an *overt act*. Forty years later historian Daniel Boorstin would call such an action a *psuedo-event*. Nowadays we'd probably call it a *media event* or a *photo opportunity*. All such terms fit under James Reston's contemporary definition of *news management*, which suggests that while that terminology has changed, the heart of the enterprise has remained the same.

As the ranks of press agents grew, newsman Silas Bent despaired. In *Ballyhoo*, published in 1929, he reported that there were an estimated five thousand publicity agencies in New York City alone and two thousand more in Washington, D.C. He

told of a study suggesting that at least 60 percent of the stories in the *New York Times* were planted by publicists. Bent published a list of industries that had stories successfully planted:

The Junior Skippers' League, which held a regatta in Central Park with 20,000 spectators, so the papers said.(This has been denounced by the Federal Trade Commission as the work of a baking powder manufacturer.)

The campaign against bobbed hair. (This was for a hairnet manufacturer.)

The hoax of a floating bootlegger's palace off New York (One of many motion picture fakes.)

The widespread advice to eat hearty breakfasts. (This was on behalf of a distributor of bacon.)

This last campaign, to promote the eating of bacon, was another overt act planned by the talented Mr. Bernays. Most people don't realize that until the 1920s bacon was far from being America's standard breakfast fare. Numerous stories featuring the elite eating bacon and testimonials from nutritionists about the value of a hearty breakfast, all orchestrated by Bernays, helped to create a permanent tradition in American eating.

She's come a long way, baby, since Edward Bernays engineered this smoking parade on behalf of his tobacco company client.

Bernays finished the decade by staging one of the largest media events to date. On behalf of his client General Electric, Bernays decided to create a commemoration of the fiftieth anniversary of the electric light. He marshalled the participation of many of the leading citizens of the day, including Henry Ford who reconstructed the original laboratory and machines used by Edison to invent the electric light. Edison himself was persuaded to return to the site and re-create the moment when the illumination came. The "Golden Jubilee of Light" was held in Dearborn, Michigan, but broadcast by radio around the world. Presidents and industrial leaders were transported to the site in a fifty-year-old locomotive that had been restored for the event. In cities all over the country smaller events were timed to correspond. The resulting news stories filled two pages of the *New York Times* index.

The Golden Jubilee of Light capped a promotion-frenzied decade that had led Silas Bent to bemoan in his book on the trade, "My inquiries have brought me to a point where I look with a credulous eye only on accounts of murder, suicide, forgery and fire. These are not publicity stunts when genuine."

More Stars Than There Are in Heaven
The slogan Howard Dietz composed for MGM

The motion picture industry matured in the twenties and began a golden era that lasted almost thirty years. The major studios—Paramount, RKO, Universal, Columbia, Warner Brothers, Fox, and MGM—were in active competition. The demand for new movies was so great they evolved a virtual factory system of production, with separate departments for each aspect of the making and marketing of films.

The aptly named exploitation departments were large, with sixty to a hundred employees each, in their heyday, and structured like newspapers. There were editors, news-gathering reporters, and special news photographers. "Planters," who specialized in various columnists and news outlets, sat around all day thinking up

**The MGM
exploitation
department**

funny lines and insider stories. Editors sent stories to the hometown newspapers of everyone involved in a movie —even the extras and the makeup artists. And certain "specialists" spent all their time thinking up ideas for publicity stunts. The majority of the ideas for attracting attention to the film went into the elaborate press books sent out to theater managers.

Howard Dietz, who was later to become the vice president of MGM, started working for Samuel Goldwyn in 1924. "I first learned about exploitation, an important aspect of the movie business, from Hunt Stromberg," Dietz wrote in his autobiography, *Dancing in the Dark*.

> I sat in his office and my bewildered ears heard him dictating a letter of advice to theater owners on how to promote a picture. "Hire an elephant from a nearby circus," he said, "and have him parade through the town." I couldn't help interrupting. "Suppose there is no circus? What does he do then?" Stromberg gave me a scornful look. "That is exploitation. You tell the theater a lot of things they can't do and let them select."

The truth was that the theaters *found* an elephant—or in extreme cases made one. They jumped feet first into the spirit of ballyhoo and competed with each other for the best publicity ideas. The theater trade publications had special exploitation sections where the best stunts competed for ink. Great stunts were often repeated across the country and exhibitors were urged to share their ideas. An ad in the November 15, 1924 *Motion Picture News* urged:

> SHOWMEN WANTED: to send in live exploitation ideas for the Exhibitors Service Bureau of Motion Picture News. The stunt which has been used in your town is no longer new, but it may be the very thing the other fellow needs.

In the teens and twenties many theaters mounted lavish "prologues" —entertainment spectaculars that roughly complemented the plots of the movies they preceded. As an additional incentive to bring out the crowds, lobbies were transformed into scenes from the movies, ushers were costumed appropriately, and giveaways and contests were held on the stage.

A perennial favorite was the lookalike contest, where audience members dressed up as their favorite movie stars. Jackie Coogan lookalike contests attracted both boys *and* girls throughout the twenties and early thirties, and Charlie Chaplin lookalikes brought out crowds of Little Tramps. Often, contest entrants were given free tickets for participating.

One theater promotion that became a revered institution began originally as a publicity stunt. On May 1, 1927, to celebrate the opening of Grauman's Chinese Theatre in Hollywood, Mary Pickford and Douglas Fairbanks made their footprints in the wet concrete outside. Thus began a tradition that has never failed to attract nationwide publicity for a star.

An historic moment is captured as Douglas Fairbanks, Jr. and Mary Pickford start a tradition in cement outside the new Grauman's Chinese Theater on Hollywood Boulevard. Sid Grauman is at far left.

More than a hundred stars have been invited to add their footprints or other parts of their anatomy. Variations on the theme have included Al Jolson's knees, Jim Durante's nose and Bette Grable's legs. Honoring stars with this type of self-created "ceremonial" has long appealed to publicity stuntsters and their clients.

To keep ideas flowing, the exploitation departments sent field publicists out to travel from city to city and advise the theater owners, helping them to launch premieres and pull off stunts. The field publicist was a direct descendant of the circus advance man, with the important difference that the circus could open in only one city at a time whereas a film opened simultaneously in hundreds or even thousands of theaters. With guidelines from the central office, the field publicists would plot strategies with the theater owners and formulate ideas for the local media. Their day was made if a locally planted stunt made the wire services and gained national coverage.

Strategy for national coverage was planned at the studio headquarters. One legendary publicity stunt of the twenties was instigated on behalf of the MGM logo. It was the brainchild of an apprentice of Harry Reichenbach, Pete Smith, who later went on to a very sucessful career producing short subjects. Smith had been brought to MGM by Howard Deitz after he'd staged a spectacular stunt for the movie *Robin Hood* involving Douglas Fairbanks, Jr. shooting arrows off a Manhattan skyscraper.

Smith's idea was inspired by the biggest story of 1927—Charles Lindbergh's solo flight across the Atlantic. After that, any story that tied-in with aviation was news. Soon publicity seekers were using aircraft to carry messages for every conceivable product, and stories of stunt flying and gimmicks—for instance, tennis playing on the wings of an airplane, changing planes in midair—filled the newspapers.

Smith's idea, to send Leo the MGM lion across the country in an airplane, was a guaranteed publicity goldmine. The studio had a special cage constructed and hired an experienced pilot. The plane took off from San Diego, California, on September 16, 1927, to great fanfare. Celebrities flocked to the site to be photographed with the maned beast and, just as Smith had anticipated, reporters from around the world gathered on the tarmac to cover the take-off.

The pilot of the fateful Leo the Lion flight checks his passenger prior to take-off

LEO
M.G.M. FLYING LION

Although heavily weighted with the lion and the cage, the plane took off from the airport without incident. But soon, the plans went awry. The plane simply disappeared. In New York, a waiting crowd of two thousand finally had to be sent home. For three days there was no word; for three days the nation feared the worst. By the time the lion and pilot turned up safe in Arizona, where the plane had gone down in a storm, cynics were certain that the disappearance had been part of the publicity stunt. MGM denied this, claiming that the deliberate hoax was a ploy of the past.

In reality, the hoax still had a few years to live in the arsenal of the publicist. Along with other forms of publicity stunts, the hoax thrived throughout the thirties. And whether MGM had staged the loss of its own lion is debated to this day.

All publicity is good, except an obituary notice.
Brendan Behan

The Depression did little to slow the publicity frenzy. In fact, a declining box office from 1929 through 1933 inspired a veritable giveaway fever among theater owners. Customers vied for prizes ranging from sets of dishes to new cars. Sid Grauman dreamed up a memorable promotion when he arranged with the Ford company to mount a car-assembly contest on the stage of his Chinese Theater. Two teams raced furiously to assemble a Model T and drive it off the stage.

Premieres of a new picture were a good handle for a stunt. A prototype for future press junkets was pulled off on behalf of the movie *42nd Street*. Warner Brothers chartered an entire train which they christened "The 42nd Street Special" and filled it with stars and reporters. The train departed Los Angeles in late February 1933 and stopped in cities along the route to New York. Stories and newsreels were filed from each location. Finally, a month later and with great fanfare, it pulled into Grand Central Station at 42nd Street, and a star-studded premiere was held the next night.

Soon the studios were transporting press contingents to various parts of the country on a regular basis. The junket became a tool of public relations people in all industries. Grand openings, plant dedications, company anniversaries, and production milestones (one million widgets!) all became excuses to bring in the reporters. After being wined and dined for several days, the reporters would usually reciprocate with stories about the company. It wasn't until the issue-conscious sixties that the morality of seducing reporters came under scrutiny.

By 1936 even *Variety* acknowledged that the exploitation departments were honing their skills and developing more sophisticated techniques of publicity. In an article entitled "PRESS AGENTRY NOW REFINED ART," it reported that, "Operation has been tightened, speeded, elaborated along specialized lines, growing away from the sometime successful but often back-firing screwball plantings of individual stunt masters toward more de-personalized institutional activities." But *Variety* was wrong. At least twenty more years of constant stunting would come out of Hollywood before television began to make inroads into the studio budgets. And several of the greatest stunt masters were still to emerge.

A press agent who worries about taste is as badly miscast as a soldier who faints at the sight of blood.

The New Yorker, from a four-part profile of Russell Birdwell, 1944

By the mid 1930s, the studios were organizing tours for drama editors from all over the country and planting national stories from Hollywood. Box office receipts had skyrocketed and the millions of dollars at stake with each film justified a continual expansion of publicity and advertising techniques.

Russell Birdwell, the head of publicity for David O. Selznick International, brought a certain legitimacy to the publicity stunt. Birdwell had been a successful journalist and producer before Selznick hired him in 1935. One of his first ideas in his new job was a fresh twist on an old gag. He arranged for a famous G-man to be hired as a guard at Selznick's studio—not to guard the possessions but to guard the ideas. The "brainguard" was news. At first, Selznick was not pleased and complained that the stunt was in poor taste. "Birdwell was disconcerted to learn that he was supposed to be a press agent and have taste too," *The New Yorker* reported. "He indignantly resigned." Selznick soon recognized his error and rehired Birdwell. "Thus," said *The New Yorker*, "Birdwell had come safely through the greatest crisis of his life. If he had allowed taste to win the upper hand, he would have never amounted to anything."

Birdwell stayed with Selznick for four years and managed to establish himself as one of the most original press agents of his day. For example, for the premiere of *The Prisoner of Zenda*, Birdwell flew the entire town of Zenda, Ontario, (population 12), to New York City. Even *Time* magazine covered this wacky stunt.

Birdwell is also credited with the spectacular *Gone with the Wind* buildup that began with its casting in 1937. The nationwide talent search for an unknown to play Scarlett was front-page news for months. The idea of a talent search wasn't new when Birdwell used it but it worked for him in a big way and it continues to this day to be a surefire news getter.

The *Gone with the Wind* premiere, which was planned not just by Birdwell but by the entire exploitation department of MGM—and many people took credit for its success—was a phenomenon that received worldwide

Thousands line the streets in front of the theater where *Gone with the Wind* premieres.

coverage. The opening of a mere movie actually pushed aside the impending news of World War II. In Atlanta, hundreds of thousands of people gathered in the streets to watch the stars arrive at the theater. Taking their cues from Edward Bernays's Golden Jubilee of Lights, publicists were learning to orchestrate publicity stunts on ever grander scales—what would eventually come to be called media events.

By the time Birdwell left Selznick to start his own publicity firm, World Publicity Corporation, he had become more famous than his stunts. *Variety* noted that "Birdwell, who came from the newspaper game to set a fast pace in the scheme of Hollywood publicity, has introduced revolutionary measures, high powered stunts, given sound advice and admonished the industry on the importance of proper publicity. He is credited by many with having raised Hollywood press agentry to a new high and made the calling an important profession."

The American Newspaper Publishers Association would have emphatically disagreed with *Variety*'s evaluation. In fact, as press agentry raged unabated throughout the thirties, the ANPA continued to fight against it. Particularly from 1935 on, they called on their members to renew their guard against press agents' material. Some newspapers responded. The Hackensack (New Jersey) *Bergen Evening Record*, for example, issued a directive that forbade the printing of press releases and declared that "any employee responsible for permitting the publication of an article contrary to this policy (of exclusion) will be billed for the offending article in full at the regular reader advertising rates."

JIM MORAN, STUNTS FOR SALE

In all of this world, there is nothing more dismal than a fact.

Jim Moran

Possibly the greatest publicity stuntster of all time burst on the scene in the late thirties. Jim Moran's career was to span four decades, from 1937 to his retirement in 1985, and over its course he worked in all industries and every medium. His stunts put him constantly in the news and he slipped onto television like he was born to it, maturing with it and becoming a master of the commercial plug. But Moran's first great idea for a publicity stunt was one that he didn't actually execute. In the early thirties, Moran co-owned an aviation company, and thought he would attract attention to it by flying over the White House and parachuting live bunny rabbits onto the lawn during the annual Easter Egg Hunt. Fortunately, cooler heads prevailed.

But Moran continued looking for ways to make his ideas airborne. Years later he was arrested in Central Park just as he was attempting to lift off a trio of midgets on kites. Each kite was printed with advertisements extolling Moran's client's products. Although the police stopped the stunt on the grounds that it was too dangerous, the coverage of the aborted plan was sufficient to warrant Moran's by-then exorbitant fee.

Moran always operated a little differently from other press agents—rather than waiting to be hired he would come up with an idea and then find a client to attach it to. Frequently he himself would enact the idea, thereby earning as much publicity for himself as for the client. His first publicity stunt to break big was his sale of a refrigerator to an Eskimo in Alaska. Moran had overheard two salesmen quoting the oft-used excuse for poor results, "You can't sell a refrigerator to an Eskimo." Lining up the American Ice Manufacturers as his client, Moran donned his winter coat and headed for the Yukon. Eventually he was able to find a buyer in an Eskimo named Charlie and with great ceremony presented the icebox. The announcement of the sale amused the world. Not one to waste an opportunity, Moran proceeded triumphantly to Hollywood with several snow-blind fleas that he sold to Paramount and with 100 pounds of glacier ice that he sold to various merchants to use in displays.

The success of the icebox stunt ensured Moran a lifetime career as a publicity stuntster. Establishing headquarters in New York City, he maintained a private costume and prop collection which he drew upon for his various stunts. Once, on behalf

Jim Moran, bundled up for his foray to Alaska in 1938 to sell an icebox to an Eskimo, managed to get the name of his sponsoring airline into the picture.

of *The Mouse That Roared*, he outfitted himself in a military uniform and posed as the Ambassador of Grand Fenwick, the mythical duchy from the film. Moran opened an official embassy for Grand Fenwick in Washington, D.C., and had himself chauffeured to diplomatic parties in a Mercedes-Benz with a sterling silver mouse as a hood ornament. He spent two weeks in Washington and culminated the charade by throwing a full-dress ball for more than five hundred people for whom he screened the forthcoming film.

Moran specialized in preposterous stunts. In fact, most of the stunts included in the preposterous acts, puns, and proverbs section of this book are his. Once, in the early forties, Moran was on retainer with Fred Waring, a well-known orchestra leader of the day who had his own radio show. Waring and his announcer, Paul Douglas, had a long-standing argument over whether California sunshine was better than Florida sunshine. Moran decided to prove the answer "scientifically." He designed a costume for himself that covered half of his body, and then spent one week in Florida tanning one side and the next week in California

**Jim Moran's right
half taking in the
Florida sun**

tanning the other side. Then, the degree of tanning was compared. The contest was followed avidly by both states' departments of tourism and Moran wisely decided to declare a tie. This ensured Waring's continued welcome at invited performances on both coasts.

When reporters heard from Jim Moran they knew they were in for a publicity stunt, but they went because they knew they would get a great story. His antics were the bane, however, of the burgeoning profession of sober-sided public relations counselors, whose influence continued to grow as the century wore on.

Publicity men have risen in little more than a generation from quacks and gold brick artists to policy makers of industry and government.
The New Yorker, 1944

Edward Bernays had spent the thirties crusading on behalf of public relations. Although he was discouraged at the slow progress of the struggle for legitimacy, he was heartened to see universities begin to offer courses in public relations and the business press to make ever-increasing references to its practitioners. However, it would take World War II to turn public relations into an accepted fixture of American life.

Both world wars were opportunities and mandates to the nations involved to use every known trick of propaganda to advance their own causes. The *New York Times* called World War I "The Press Agents War." Even the notorious hoaxer Harry Reichenbach was called upon to employ his fertile mind on behalf of the Allies. Government information offices used press releases, a public relations invention, to pass information to the eager hordes of journalists. Thus, the press grew accustomed to accepting "handouts" and to relying more and more on press agents and public relations professionals as news sources.

Throughout the thirties, government itself began to "manage the news," carefully setting up press bureaus in every one of its departments through which to channel and control information. Reporters found it increasingly difficult to talk directly to government officials and had to be content with the official handouts.

President Roosevelt was a master of publicity and used all forms of the media to get his message out. "Knowing that newspapermen lived on news, he helped them manufacture

Fala, President Roosevelt's pet Scottie, listens to his master's trademark fireside chat. Presidential pets offer a traditional photo opportunity.

it," wrote historian Daniel Boorstin in his book *Image*. "And he knew enough about newsmaking techniques to help shape their stories to his own purposes."

At that time radio was the primary communications vehicle and Roosevelt used it well. His "fireside chats," the president's addresses to the nation, were examples of "psuedo events," defined by Boorstin as events created to make news.

World War II was a renewed opportunity to test the power of propaganda. This time our government openly engaged the services of the entertainment community to create films and documentaries promoting the Allied cause. Hollywood film stars led the effort to raise money for war bonds and the admission prices to many premieres were donated to the war effort. *Yankee Doodle Dandy* alone raised $30 million through premieres in a number of cities, and President Roosevelt presented Jack Warner with a special award for service.

Two centuries ago when a great man appeared, people looked for God's purpose in him; today we look for his press agent.
Daniel Boorstin

Since World War II, public relations has experienced a spectacular growth. The number of practitioners in 1950 was estimated at 20,000; By 1987 that number had increased sevenfold to an estimated 142,000. The actual number at any time is considered to be at least twice that reported, because practitioners work under so many different titles it is difficult to get an accurate count. The 1980s name for public relations is *corporate communications*. Jack O'Dwyer, publisher of the *Directory of Corporate Communications*, stated that only about 30 percent of the companies listed still use the term *public relations*, while *corporate communications* or just plain *communi-*

cations is used by nearly 20 percent. *Corporate relations, public information,* and *public affairs* are other titles currently in use.

Hundreds of new public relations agencies have sprung up and 87 percent those now in business were founded since World War II. In the corporate sector, thousands of new jobs have been created. Corporate communications is the fastest growing segment of the public relations industry.

What accounts for this amazing proliferation? Many observers attribute it to the consumer movement of the sixties which catapulted Ralph Nader and his followers to national importance. The consumer movement introduced people to the idea that the average person can use the media to gain access to power. More and more people did just that, and in response, the powerful corporations redoubled their own media manipulations. As at the turn of the century, when businesses responded to muckrakers' attacks by developing public relations programs, in the sixties, corporations responded to consumer attacks the same way—by beefing up their public relations departments.

THE NEWS EXPLOSION

There is no news, there's only media.
Susan Halas

Another primary factor in the growth of public relations was the advent of television in the late 1940s and the corresponding media explosion that caused us to become a true "information society." In 1909 there were 2,600 daily newspapers with a combined circulation of 24 million. In 1987, the number of daily newspapers had dropped to 1,677, but their combined circulation had more than doubled, to 64 million. In addition there were 7,600 weeklies with a combined circulation of 47,593,000 and hundreds of national magazines, including 72 with circulations topping a million. (Together, those 72 magazines had more than 200 million readers.)

And as the outlets for news have grown so has the number of reporters. At the 1988 Democratic Convention, twelve thousand reporters crammed the hall. There were three reporters for every delegate! Everywhere this massive media menagerie voraciously scavenges for news, never satiated and never sleeping.

Humorist Dave Barry made the point succinctly when he and several companions put cardboard boxes on their heads and paraded outside the convention hall housing the 1988 Democratic convention. This was a test to see how long it would take the media to converge. The answer: seven seconds.

It was television that accounted in large part for this massive growth. The first national news broadcast originated in New York in 1949. In the fifties television news was of slight importance and of slighter quality. But in 1963 network evening news expanded from fifteen minutes to half an hour and that year for the first time more people listed television than newspapers as their chief source of news. Also that year, the nation sat mesmerized for four days watching round-the-clock coverage of the Kennedy assassination. Television had become the common thread of experience for the majority.

By 1988 television had created a global news network—more than 750 million television sets in 160 countries were being watched by an estimated 2.5 billion people. More people today have access to television than to telephones. In 1835, the French observer Alexis de Tocqueville wrote, "The newspaper is the only instrument by which the same thought can be dropped into a thousand minds at the same moment." Today the same thought can be dropped into a billion minds at the same moment.

*In New York you can
get the Press faster
than you can get
the cops.*
Abbie Hoffman

People with something to say to
the world came to understand the
potential of staging events for television. The leaders of the civil rights
movement tapped this mine of influence using, for example, sit-ins and
carefully planned marches. Following
their model, the radical student
leaders of the sixties quickly learned
how to translate a grass-roots protest
into a powerful media event, a living,
moving image that could add life to
the words of television's typical
talking heads.

Many movements of the sixties co-
opted the publicity stunt to put their
messages to the nation, and some,
particularly the radical war protesters
known as the Yippies, became masters
of the outrageous. Yippie leader Abbie
Hoffman called their media strategies
gorilla warfare. In an interview in
Pranks!, a special issue of *Re/Search*
magazine published in 1987, he recalls
the time when twenty Yippies threw
dollar bills from the gallery of the
stock exchange and stopped trading
for about six minutes. Although the
incident made the news, there was no
picture because, Hoffman said, "At
that time we didn't quite have the
concept of media events down." But
by 1968, an election year, the Yippies
had learned how to plan a stunt for
optimum coverage. They brought a
live pig to the Democratic convention
in Chicago and presented it as the
Yippie presidential candidate. As Paul
Krassner later reminisced in *Pranks!*,
"It was a good media scene. In fact,
the secret of the Yippies was: we got
millions and millions of dollars of free
publicity on TV because we were
providing more *stimulating theater*."

Providing stimulating theater for the television cameras quickly became the modus operandi of protest groups. Massing a group of sign-carrying demonstrators at a specific location, perhaps getting arrested, became a routine method of ensuring media coverage. Variations on that theme—such as underground personality Wavy Gravy disguising himself as a Mutant Bunny at a protest against a nuclear power plant, or a human chain stretching across America to highlight world hunger—all operate on the same principle.

Journalist Tom Wolfe tells the story of witnessing a crowd of demonstrators approach a camera crew to ask, "What should we do?" The symbiotic relationship of news to newsmakers has never been stronger.

The black and white Pigasus ("the integrated candidate") was brought to Chicago from California's Hog Farm Commune to run as the 1968 Yippie presidential candidate.

THE END OF AN ERA

The one thing about movie stunts for publicity purposes, you can't write a textbook on this. It's impossible because every picture has a different reason for being.

Marty Weiser

Television had a negative impact on Hollywood. As TV secured its audience, movie production declined and with it the studio system and the studios' massive exploitation departments. Nowadays stars hire their own press agents, and many of Hollywood's most successful public relations firms have become international businesses with the largest percentage of their clients being the lucrative corporate accounts. By 1988 the Publicist's Guild had only 510 members, and 100 of them were out of work.

Many of the guild members and other industry old-timers attended the funeral that year of Marty Weiser, who at age seventy-six was one of the last of the great publicity stuntsters. Weiser, a behind-the-scenes genius who truly delighted in dreaming up stunts, had worked for Warner Brothers for fifty years. It was Weiser, I discovered, who turned the theater into the gigantic Easter bonnet that had so impressed me as a child.

Today Hollywood publicity departments are no longer called exploitation departments. Most studios hire marketing directors with backgrounds in advertising who generally eschew the old-time Hollywood ballyhoo. But Weiser, working long hours in a tiny, cluttered office, kept the tradition alive. He regarded every film, no matter what its quality, as worthy of a wholehearted effort and some of the stunts he thought up in his final years were his most memorable.

In an interview taped in 1987, Weiser recalled his own personal favorite and the stunt that brought the biggest reaction. "The picture was *Blazing Saddles*, an outrageous comedy, if you remember, a spoof on all the westerns that were ever made, a very funny picture. Now, how do you do a stunt for a picture like that? You come up with an outrageous idea. So I had a special premiere for horses—a screening for horses, and we went through all the motions that we do on a screening for people." The premiere was held at a drive-in theater in Los Angeles near a bunch of horse stables. Weiser put a small ad in the *Los Angeles Times* "calling all horses"—inviting the horses and their "friends" to a special screening at the drive-in. At the last minute, concerned that horsepeople might not read the *Times*, he tacked flyers on trees in nearby parks. "And then I prayed that somebody would show up," Weiser recalled. "If just half a dozen horses showed up, it would be a success, in my mind. And the press really loved

Horsing around at the *Blazing Saddles* premiere

this idea so everybody was there—all the networks, seven local stations, the columnists, radio commentators—it was amazing, the media turnout was tremendous. And all of us are just sitting there waiting. At an empty drive-in."

Just as Weiser began to fear that nobody would show up, a police motorcycle drove in. "And I'm wondering, am I in trouble, are they coming after me?" However, the policeman was merely the escort for a veritable parade of horses and their riders. More than 250 showed up to fill the drive-in, each one standing in a car space next to a sound-hookup pole. At the snack bar, Weiser had set up a "horsepitality bar" offering oats in popcorn buckets and other "horse d'oevres." The coverage of the event, which was worldwide, was wildly successful. The screening achieved a level of preposterousness that most stuntsters only dream of.

Weiser's imagination had always had a nutty edge. As a field representative in Kansas in 1939, he arranged for the teamsters to donate a twenty-ton truck to Ann Sheridan, and to designate her "the girl we'd most like to give a lift to." This was a stunt on behalf of *They Drive by Night*, a now-forgotten potboiler about a couple of truck drivers and their girlfriends. Weiser supervised the cross-country delivery of the truck, which stopped in each major market where a convoy of local dignitaries would autograph its side. Even presidential candidate Wendell Willkie made a special detour to get in on the "photo opportunity" with the truck. When the truck finally arrived in Hollywood, it was presented to Sheridan in an appropriate ceremony.

The story had a sad ending, Weiser recalled, when he got ready to return the truck. Sheridan, having believed the publicity, thought the truck was actually hers and had promised it to her brother. She cried when Weiser had to tell her it was just a publicity stunt.

Once Weiser even had a great idea for another studio and couldn't resist helping to pull it off. Twentieth Century Fox had planned a premiere in

San Francisco for *Hello Frisco Hello*. The theater manager was a friend of Weiser's and confided that he couldn't think of any special promotions. But when Weiser heard the title he knew what to do immediately. Knowing how much San Franciscans hated the nickname "Frisco," he suggested that the San Francisco board of supervisors be persuaded to ban the movie. Working behind the scenes, he got the mayor of San Francisco to make a special trip to Los Angeles to meet with Darryl Zanuck, then head of Twentieth Century Fox, to register a complaint about the title. With great fanfare, the studio agreed to change the title for viewing in San Francisco and actually changed the opening credits on the film and in all the Bay Area ads to read *Hello San Francisco Hello*. Elsewhere in the nation, though, it remained *Hello Frisco Hello*. The stunt was such a success that the theater manager was promoted, but Weiser couldn't talk about it for years thinking that Warner Brothers wouldn't appreciate his slipping such a great idea to a rival studio.

Weiser approached every movie fresh, looking for an idea.

"There's always some angle," he said, "It's the star, it's the picture, it's the story, and you have to do a lot of thinking. And then you never know, not all of them work." He had probably hit on a major reason for the decline of the publicity stunt over the last two decades among many public relations people. There's a lot of work involved with no guarantee of results. If a major news story overshadows the stunt, the time and money will have been wasted.

The publicity stunt has survived, but as the more genteel "media event." This evolution reflects the tremendous gain in legitimacy and power public relations as a profession has attained. We're living in what is being called the Golden Age of Public Relations, in which practitioners use multiple techniques and technologies to help them pitch and plant clients' stories. It is now possible to produce a videotape for a client and see it run on the television news as a news story (this is the so-called video press release). The television station saves crew and camera time, the public relations agency controls the message, and the viewer can't tell the difference. PR firms now commission national opinion polls on behalf of clients, fax stories into newspaper offices, and control their own wire and photography services. In the face of this "bold new superhype," as this PR style has been called, the publicity stunt seems dated and a little quaint.

Still, there will always be a use for the clever idea that just has to break its way into the news. The whole world smiled in 1988 when a New York television station took a Gorbachev lookalike on a limousine tour of Manhattan while the real Gorbachev was meeting with President Reagan. The lookalike drew huge, excited crowds, but the delicious climax occurred when the self-important but apparently gullible real estate magnate Donald Trump actually broke through the crowd with his bodyguards to shake the impostor's hand. This was a stunt that proved irresistible despite the professed "maturity" and "sophistication" of both the PR and media worlds. Trump's faux pas attracted global attention and the whole world got a good laugh.

This book is meant as a remembrance and a celebration of P.T. Barnum, Harry Reichenbach, Russell Birdwell, Jim Moran, Marty Weiser, and those who followed the trail they blazed. Their best stunts plus the brainchildren of many who learned from them or were inspired out of their own madcap imaginations are described in the following pages. Here's hoping such outrageous acts never disappear and that we never lose our ability to enjoy them.

Chapter 2

Flimflammery and Ballyhooliganism
The Great Hoaxes and Hoaxers

I like publicity. I like to watch it operate. When I was bored, I used to drop into the publicity office at Warner Bros. and invent stories. I invented a story about Paul Muni's beard to the effect that Muni had a beard room and that he left the window open and all the beards flew into the ocean. The story got printed.

Humphrey Bogart

One of the biggest stories of 1988 was the revelation that a couple of actors had hoaxed the top television talk shows. The woman claimed to be a sex surrogate, while her male accomplice described himself as an aging virgin. Both gave false names and convincing performances. When the hoax was exposed, the story made the front pages of newspapers around the country. The hoaxed hosts were outraged and indignant. Oprah Winfrey complained that people would no longer know whom to trust. The way the story was reported made such an incident seem unusual, but, as shown in the preceding chapter, hoaxing has a long and hallowed tradition in American journalism.

"By far a majority of the fake stories that are pulled over the desk, originate with or are produced in collaboration with the newspaper that floats the fake," reported *Editor & Publisher* in 1907. "There are certain newspapers that prefer an interesting fake to a true story."

As a general rule, however, most hoaxes did not originate with journalists. From Barnum onward, the hoax was a staple in the press agents' repertory. Faked disappearances, stolen jewelry, hairbreadth escapes from death, and staged elopements were all tried and true headline getters. Until New York district attorney Swann's investigation in the twenties, nobody seemed to mind.

One of the earliest publicity stunt hoaxes was pulled off in 1809 by Washington Irving, best remembered today for his *Legend of Sleepy Hollow*. Irving formulated an elaborate plan to launch his book *Knickerbocker's History of New York*. First, he planted a story in the *New York Evening Post* about the disappearance of a man named Knickerbocker from his room at a New York hotel. Several days later it was reported that the hotel manager had found a lengthy manuscript in the missing man's room. The management threatened to sell the writings to cover unpaid bills if Knickerbocker didn't show up. All this was duly reported. A month after the "disappearance," Inskeep and Bradford, Irving's publisher, announced the forthcoming publication of *Knickerbocker's History of New York*.

Hoaxers pose with "creature" on a beach near Ballard, Washington in 1906. Publicizing alleged sightings of sea serpents was a favorite strategy of press agents employed by seaside resorts.

NOBODY THERE

The "missing person" was always a dependable newsmaker, and easy to pull off in the days before global communications made disappearing more difficult. A variation, the "non-existent person" had its own successes. In the early 1940s press agent Dave Epstein drove reporters wild with his continued press releases about the activities of a "Ned Farrington." Farrington, allegedly an important New York producer, was constantly signing Epstein's clients to prestigious projects. In 1942 the *New York Times* reported that Ned Farrington was "an elusive Broadway producer who is forever reported to be holding conversations with Hollywood writers, producers and directors. . . . Several correspondents have tried to check Farrington stories without success. He's usually traveling between New York and Hollywood." Farrington stories continued to be printed for about ten years. Finally, Jim Henagan, a columnist for

the *Hollywood Reporter*, decided he had had enough and announced Farrington's death. The *Daily Variety* followed up with a detailed account of Farrington's funeral. Their efforts didn't stop Epstein for long, however. Soon press releases were pouring in about the activities of one "Choteau Fresnay," whose activities in Europe on behalf of Epstein's clients kept them in the public eye continually. Readers of all these items, of course, had no idea of the behind-the-scenes shenanigans and presumably took the stories at face value.

Public trances and fainting fits, especially as suffered by nubile young women, have always fallen under suspicion as hoaxers' handiwork. Harry Reichenbach used the trance to publicize the silent movie *Trilby* which starred Clara Kimball Young. In the movie, Young's character becomes mesmerized, and at the premiere screening Reichenbach planted a young girl who apparently fell into a trance along with the character. When the movie ended she remained motionless, her eyes glazed. She was rushed to a nearby hospital where her trance held for twelve hours. While specialists examined her, reporters interviewed psychologists about the trance phenomenon.

Professors from Harvard and Princeton opined that it was indeed possible for a susceptible person to be hypnotized by a movie, and moviegoers were warned to be careful when they watched *Trilby*. All this had a marvelous effect on the box office, of course. In his book *Phantom Fame*, Reichenbach recalled that "the only catalepsy the girl suffered from was that she wanted a screen career which I promised her if the stunt went through."

Many years later Marty Weiser used a similar ruse to draw attention to *The Exorcist*. He claimed he saw a person faint after rushing out of a theater showing the film; then he invited reporters to attend a screening. Sure enough, someone else passed out at the press screening. Nurses and ambulances, provided free of charge by the studio, were standing by.

A rash of fainting in the audience of "The Phil Donahue" show occurred soon after the TV talk show changed locations from Chicago to New York. Alan Abel, a self-described freelance media hoaxer, claimed responsibility for this hoax. In an interview in *Pranks!*, he told of receiving a call from one of Donahue's assistants, who allegedly said, "It's very important that Phil's new show gets good ratings in New York. Why don't you come up with some media stunt, and if it works, and doesn't kill anybody or hurt anybody, you'll be well paid." Abel decided to hire actors to pretend to faint in the audience. The swoonings caused near pandemonium among the healthy audience members; some even feared they were witnessing an outbreak of Legionnaire's disease. Eventually Donahue cleared the studio and continued the show without an audience. The story of the "unaccountable faintings" generated over six thousand press reports the world over. The show's ratings did skyrocket, but there is no evidence that Donahue himself was in on the hoax.

Planting people in an audience to influence response is as old as the claques of the ancient Greeks. One of the most successful audience manipulations ever was the brainstorm of one of Frank Sinatra's early press agents, George Evans. Kitty Kelley tells the story in *His Way*, her unauthorized biography of Sinatra. Evans, a highly successful entertainment press agent, attended one of Sinatra's concerts and saw one girl throw a rose at Frank and another girl moan a little. "I thought if I could fill the theatre with a bunch of girls moaning, 'Oh, Frankie,' I've got something there," Evans reminisced. Accordingly, he hired a group of girls and paid them five dollars each to jump and scream and yell "Oh, Frankie! Oh, Frankie!" when Sinatra sang a slow song.

He drilled them in the basement of the Paramount, directing them to holler when Frank bent and dipped certain notes. "They shouldn't only yell and squeal, they should fall apart," Evans said. . . . Two of the girls were coached to fall in a dead faint in the aisle, while the others were told to moan in unison as loudly as they could.

The scheme succeeded beyond anyone's wildest dreams. The theater was filled to capacity with schoolkids on vacation who had received free passes from Evans. Ushers carried bottles of ammonia, and an ambulance was parked outside. Evans had alerted a few selected columnists and photographers, and the next day pictures of girls being carried out unconscious appeared in all the papers.

"We hired girls to scream when he sexily rolled a note," said Jack Keller, who was George Evans's partner on the West Coast. "The dozen girls we hired to scream and swoon did exactly as we told them. But hundreds more we didn't hire screamed even louder. Others squealed, howled, kissed his pictures with their lipsticked lips, and kept him a prisoner in his dressing room between shows at the Paramount. It was wild, crazy, completely out of control."

From that point on Sinatra was a national phenomenon. Wherever he appeared, screaming girls would follow. Hundreds of stories were written about the hysteria, with Evans fanning the flames. Influencing mass behavior in this way seemed alarmingly easy.

An audience of screamers at a Frank Sinatra concert in 1944 included "plants" paid by Sinatra's press agent to feign hysteria.

MAKING THE NEWS

An invented story launched the careers of both movie legend Rita Hayworth and her press agent, Henry Rogers. Rogers, the founder of one of the world's most successful public relations agencies, Rogers and Cowan, was a cub press agent back in 1939 when he was approached by the then-unknown starlet. Hayworth was under contract to Columbia, but her career had gone nowhere and she needed a publicity break to get the studio to take her seriously. In his autobiography, *Walking the Tightrope*, Rogers tells how he got her that break.

First he told Gene Herrick, the West Coast editor of *Look* magazine that Hayworth had just been proclaimed the best-dressed off-screen actress of 1939 by the "Fashion Couturiers of America." His client spent every cent of her annual $15,000 salary on her wardrobe, Rogers said, and the award proved that her efforts had paid off. This so impressed Herrick that he assigned a photographer to shoot some pictures for *Look*.

Before the photographer arrived, Rogers was a very busy man. In just a few days time he had to round up a wardrobe that looked like $15,000 a year. Not only was there no Fashion Couturiers Association, but Hayworth's closet was pretty bare. By begging and borrowing, Rogers was able to assemble some impressive ensembles—impressive enough to put Rita Hayworth on the cover and inside nine pages of the February 27, 1940 issue of *Look*. The coverage made Hayworth a star and confirmed Rogers's natural talent for his work.

Today, the media glut would make a cover story on one magazine insufficient to launch a star, but the same angle with some refinement could still be effective. The modern press agent would need to contact an actual fashion organization and convince it to issue an award to his or her client. There would be a fine line there between a hoax and a legitimate stunt. In the old days there didn't have to be any line at all. Rogers summed up the modern approach in *Walking the Tightrope*: "Today. . . the experienced press agent would cover his tracks. He would never put himself in the position of being caught in an apparent lie. He would not try to make up news, concoct it, dream it up and invent it out of pure imagination. Instead he would actually go out and make the news."

This 1947 photo of Marilyn Monroe, taken when she was eighteen years old, alleged to be an impromptu shot of her at work. Few remember that Monroe's early studio biography claimed she was discovered while babysitting for a casting agent. Twentieth Century Fox press agent Jet Fore, who invented the story, killed it at Monroe's request after *Gentlemen Prefer Blondes* made her a star.

FOOLING THE PRESS FOR FUN

Alan Abel, the freelance media hoaxer who staged the "Donahue" fainting epidemic, is not a press agent but likes to think up ways to fool the media for the sheer fun of it. "On a slow newsday," he told *Pranks!*, "I like to jump in and create some havoc, in between the axe murders and the hostage taking." Once he even staged his own death and got an obituary in the *New York Times*. His most successful hoax was his nationwide campaign to clothe naked animals, which attracted ongoing coverage over many months. The *San Francisco Chronicle* ran a front-page series on the hilarious but poker-faced campaign.

In 1962, Abel formed The Society for Indecency to Naked Animals, (SINA), which had an official letterhead, a newsletter, a board of directors, a theme song, a membership card, and free patterns for animal garments. SINA claimed to have a membership of almost forty thousand and funds of $400,000. The president, a G. Clifford Prout, Jr., toured the country on behalf of the group.

In San Francisco, Prout and his assistants (one being Abel, who identified himself as the paid vice president of the organization) reportedly found the city to be a "major 'moral disaster area' because it tolerates so many naked animals." "Shocked" by the nudity of the animals at the Children's Petting Zoo in Golden Gate Park, the crusaders attempted to garb a reluctant fawn. According to the *Chronicle*, the onlooking children "screamed with joy and one little boy fell off the fence laughing as the three SINA executives tried unsuccessfully to hitch a pair of white panties on Bambi's hindquarters."

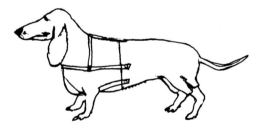

Sketch from SINA press kit

On page one, the *Chronicle* ran illustrations of the "free patterns" SINA offered to those wishing to make outfits for their animals. These included bikinis for stallions, half-slips for cows, boxer shorts for certain small animals, and knickers for bulldogs. The paper's series was written in a humorous style, but seemed to accept SINA as a bona fide movement. Actually, according to a source on the *Chronicle* staff at the time, the management was well aware that this was a hoax but ran it because it was such a good story. The SINA series certainly worked to generate reader reaction. Not long after it appeared, the newspaper ran an entire page of letters to the editor about the campaign. No announcement of a hoax ever appeared, although the paper did run an item months later noting that G. Clifford Prout was actually Buck Henry and that Henry had been hired as a comedy writer for the "Gary Moore Show."

The patterns for dog and cat bloomers that appeared in the *San Francisco Chronicle*.

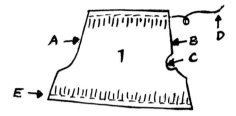

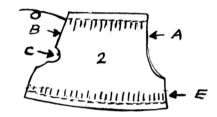

SINA pattern #69-D

Dog and/or cat BLOOMERS
(Small, medium, large)

1. Left leg
2. Right leg
A. Sew (A) sides together
B. Sew (B) sides together
C. Opening for tail
D. Draw string through waist band
   to gather and tie
E. Elastic through leg band
   to gather

Meanwhile "Prout" continued his media tour, appearing on "The Tonight Show," "The Today Show," and "The Tomorrow Show." According to Abel, everyone took it very seriously. "For me this was a proving ground, " he told *Pranks!*, "I realized that Buck or I could walk into any television studio with a drawing of a horse wearing bermuda shorts under our arm, and go right on the air, whether television or radio, and practically stop the show. The network news programs were all interested in these 'moral maniacs' who wanted to clothe animals."

The hoax continued into the fall of 1963, when a large group of SINA "members" picketed the White House to protest the naked horses being ridden by First Lady Jacqueline Kennedy and her daughter Caroline. This generated another round of nationwide publicity. Ultimately Abel parlayed the experience into a book contract with Simon and Schuster and went on to perform many other hoaxes. He had his wife pose as a Jewish grandmother and run for president; he announced the World Sex Olympics, with couples competing for points on style and endurance; he staged the wedding of an Idi Amin lookalike; and he fooled the *Washington Post* by passing off a man as the elusive "Deep Throat" of the Watergate scandal.

Still an active hoaxer in the late 1980s, Abel told *Pranks!* that his motive was to give people a "kick in the intellect." "Any media attention is an opportunity to perform on-camera before a network audience without having to audition for producers who normally wouldn't let you through the door (not that they're necessarily even worthy to shine your shoes). And improvisation is what life's about!"

Joey Skaggs is an artist who claims the media as his own. Skaggs is a social commentator; his goal is to illustrate how the media manipulate the news and frequently print stories without checking facts, and how easy it is for anyone to gain access to the media. The image of the media as guardian of the truth is threatened by an activist like Skaggs. "So, having created history, how can you believe in history?" asks Skaggs.

One of Skagg's best hoaxes was the "Cathouse for Dogs" which began with a classified ad in the *Village Voice:*

CATHOUSE FOR DOGS
featuring a savory selection of hot bitches. From pedigree (Fifi the French Poodle) to mutts (Lady the Tramp). Handler and Vet on duty. Stud and photo service available. No weirdos, please. Dogs only. By appointment. Call 254-7878.

After placing this ad, Skaggs staged a "night in a cathouse for dogs" just for the media. Thirty of his actor friends brought dogs, and Skaggs acted as commentator in an exhibition of the female dogs supposedly available to the male dog clientele. A beautiful woman and her saluki, both dressed in red sweaters and bows, paraded before the assembly as the watching males strained at their leashes.

The ensuing stories led to protests by the ASPCA and an indictment against Skaggs for cruelty to animals. He had to bring his friends into the district attorney's office to prove that the "cathouse" never existed—the D. A.'s staff just couldn't believe the media would cover such an event if weren't authentic. But the story had actually become part of an ABC news documentary that was nominated for an Emmy before the embarrassed producers realized they'd been had.

Another great hoax perpetrated by Skaggs resulted in an appearance on "Good Morning America," then the top-rated morning talk show in America. Skaggs professed to be Joe Bones, leader of the Fat Squad, a group of commandos who, for $300 a day (with a three-day minimum), would move into a client's home and physically restrain him or her from eating. On the show, Skaggs wore dark glasses and a hat printed with "Fat Squad." At one point the "Good Morning America" host David Hartman asked Bones, "Are you serious?" When assured he was, Hartman pronounced the group "legitimate, then." Once again a platoon of actors assisted

Skaggs. One woman posed as a client and testified that, thanks to the Fat Squad, she had lost one hundred pounds. The squad itself, a tough-looking group of men and women wearing "Fat Squad" hats and t-shirts, stood menacingly in the background.

Many newspapers were also taken in. The *Washington Post*, the *Philadelphia Inquirer*, the *Miami Herald*, the *New York Daily News,* and several wire services covered the story. When the hoax was exposed, few papers printed retractions. An embarassed David Hartman did confess to his audience that he'd been tricked, but failed to mention that Skaggs had been his guest less than a year before, that time as the designer of condominiums for fish.

Skaggs struck again in 1988 with "ClamScam." In Seattle to appear on a television show to talk about hoaxing, the native New Yorker was deeply impressed by the sight of that area's indigenous "geoducks," long-necked clams with a comical resemblance to the male reproductive organ. He was inspired to mount a "Save the Geoduck" campaign, in which, posing as a Dr. Long, he claimed that the geoduck, having been consumed as an aphrodisiac in Asia, was becoming an endangered species.

Staging a rally in front of the Japan Society in New York City to decry the slaughter of the geoduck, the hoaxer convinced the local NBC affiliate, United Press International, the German magazine *Der Spiegel,* and a group of Japanese newspapers that the clam had been eaten nearly into extinction by sex-crazed Japanese sushi lovers. Though the geoduck is neither an aphrodisiac nor endangered, the media fell for this one completely.

None of Skaggs's hoaxes attracted anything like the furor of the aforementioned hoaxers who appeared on the talk shows late in 1988 posing as sex surrogate and virgin, but Skaggs may nevertheless have found a way to have the last word. He accepted an invitation from "Entertainment Tonight" to discuss that particular hoax. An interview was taped and aired nationally in September, 1988. Only one problem: the person claiming to be Joey Skaggs, wasn't. Even though Skaggs had appeared on "Entertainment Tonight" in the past, no one noticed that the person they were interviewing was an impostor. When reached the next day to comment, Skaggs merely asked, "What did they expect?"

Chapter 3
Street Bally
Sparking a Crowd

You cannot make a man by standing a sheep on its hind legs. But by standing a flock of sheep in that position you can make a crowd of men.

Max Beerbohm, 1880

Street bally, the ancient art of attracting a crowd, can range from simply a man-in-a-sandwich-board to elaborate, fully choreographed and outlandish schemes. P. T. Barnum perfected many techniques of this outdoor ballyhoo that were adopted by other press agents and passed down through the generations. One favorite that became a classic might not be very effective today. Barnum would hire a man to walk through a crowd carrying two bricks. The man would lay down first one brick and then the other. Next, he would pick up the first and move it ahead of the second. In this fashion, by leapfrogging the two bricks, he would create a trail leading to the entrance of Barnum's show. The crowd would follow, trying to figure the logic of these actions.

A theatrical press agent with the exotic name of Toxen Worm became famous for a stunt he devised for Mrs. Patrick Campbell, a leading actress at the turn of the century. Mrs. Campbell had come over from England to perform in New York, and the story was that her delicate sensibilities were disturbed by the cacophony of the New York streets. One day, workmen began strewing tanbark on the streets and curbs around the theatre where Mrs. Campbell was appearing. On-lookers were mystified. A crowd gathered. Soon the actress arrived in a carriage and entered the theater. It was then announced that the tanbark was meant to muffle the outside noises. This made a good story for the New York papers and ensured a large attendance at Mrs. Campbell's performances.

This woodcut depicts the walnut carriage that conveyed one of P. T. Barnum's lesser known performers, Commander Nutt. Barnum's specially built carriages for his midgets drew crowds wherever they traveled.

REICHENBACH'S BALLYHOO

Harry Reichenbach, thanks to his carnival training, was a real master of street bally. Some of his devices were very simple. To attract attention to a store, he'd cover a barrel with wire netting and put a small sign on the side of the barrel reading "Danger, Snakes." Or he'd put an empty fish tank full of water in a store window with a sign saying "Invisible Fish." A concealed fan would cause the water to ripple. Once he tied up traffic in Times Square by having shapely young women in artists' smocks and berets stand on a scaffold above 42nd Street painting a huge display sign advertising one of his client's productions.

Reichenbach devised more elaborate schemes as well. To promote a play called *Over the Hill*, he hired teams of actors to dress in evening clothes and walk the theater district between 42nd and 50th Streets. One couple would state that they were on their way to see *Over the Hill* and the other couple would try to argue them out of it. Soon hundreds of people within earshot would be hearing about *Over the Hill*.

This same strategy was employed more than fifty years later by Ed and Michael Gifford, a husband and wife team publicizing Doug Henning's *The Magic Show* on Broadway. They hired thirty unemployed actors to ride up and down the elevators of major New York department stores talking loudly about Henning's show.

Probably Harry Reichenbach's most memorable street bally was employed on behalf of silent movie star Francis X. Bushman. Bushman wanted a raise and asked Reichenbach for help. This was in the early twenties when the movie studios were still headquartered in New York. Reichenbach's strategy was simple: he took Bushman on a stroll through the streets of New York to the studio headquarters. As they walked he dropped hundreds of pennies behind them. By the time the pair had arrived at their destination a huge crowd was trailing. The studio heads were surprised and greatly impressed by the size of Bushman's following, and Bushman got his raise.

Specially outfitted vehicles, such as the dual-control car advertising Mueller Auto Repair (above), and the prize fight on a truck (below), are typical of the countless ballyhoos long paraded down the streets of America.

In Louisville, Kentucky, a strongman on a bed of nails prepares to demonstrate his stamina. Next, the truck drove over the board lying on his stomach. This was a free preview of his evening act.

A street filled with sofas by a furniture store made a great promotional shot.

A trapeze artist was hired to swing from a pair of trousers, billed "the world's strongest pair of pants," in a Louisville, Kentucky, department store window.

As Francis X. Bushman proved with his pennies, the giveaway is a simple but effective way of attracting a crowd. All that's needed is the booty to give away; finding the takers is no problem. Consider the giveaway staged by the Learning Annex, an adult school headquartered in New York City. School officials announced they would drop $10,000 from the eighty-sixth story of the Empire State Building to celebrate the enrollment of the school's one-hundred-thousandth student.

When two men from the school arrived at the building entrance carrying large garbage bags full of cash, a huge crowd awaited them. The situation quickly became dangerous when the mob surged forward, and riot police had to be called to protect the would-be benefactors. Authorities at the Empire State Building were incensed and moved quickly to abort the stunt. Ultimately, the Learning Annex took solace in their headlines and donated the giveaway money to charity.

In a more orderly example, a "Mad Money Sweepstakes" to celebrate the completion of San Francisco's Embarcadero Center, an upscale shopping mall, attracted some thirty thousand participants, who lined up to get the free gift vouchers—all hoping to draw the top voucher of $1,000, which had to be spent in one hour. The winner was followed by reporters on his shopping spree and his purchases at the various establishments were reported one by one. Covered by all the major San Francisco media, the giveaway was well planned to give a detailed view of the shopping center.

DRIVING CRAZY

Even in jaded New York the sight of an orangutan driving a cab could get attention. Jim Moran was behind this wacky stunt—in this case, literally—hiding in the back seat where the actual controls had been moved. Hired by producer David Merrick to come up with something for his new play, *The Matchmaker*, Moran obtained a London cab that he had specially altered. Then he dressed the orangutan in a chauffeur's suit and cap and put him behind the wheel of the cab. The roof and both sides of the vehicle were emblazoned with placards proclaiming, "I'm on my way to *The Matchmaker*."

Moran, controlling the vehicle from the back seat, misjudged a turn, and rammed into another taxi. Fortunately no one was hurt.

Street bally is still an important marketing tool today. However, now the publicist wants the stunt to attract a television crew to reach a much larger audience. People are so used to seeing odd sights in the street these days that it takes something pretty unusual to attract a crowd.

Orangutan at the
wheel

Chapter 4
Man Hatches Egg
Preposterous Acts, Puns, and Proverbs

When a dog bites a man that is not news, but when a man bites a dog—that is news.

John B. Bogart, Editor, New York Sun, 1880

Many publicity stunts succeed because the ideas themselves are so witty or offbeat they are irresistible to journalists. One of the most famous in this genre was conceived by the master, Jim Moran. On behalf of the 1946 film *The Egg and I*, the great stuntster sat on an ostrich egg until it hatched. The feat took nineteen days, four hours, and thirty-two minutes to accomplish. This transpired on a Los Angeles ostrich farm, where a pair of ostriches named Joe and Eve reputedly had abandoned the egg. Wearing an elaborate ostrich costume created for him by a Hollywood dress designer, Moran sat in a specially constructed wheelchair with a basket hanging under the seat. At night he slept in an ostrich corral outfitted with a customized bed that enabled him to rest his posterior lightly on the egg. Throughout the entire incubation period he charged visitors fifty cents each for the privilege of watching him hatch the egg. More than fifteen hundred people came daily—much to Moran's supposed disgust. "They ought to be home doing something worthwhile," he declared. Nevertheless, when the baby ostrich finally hatched, Moran was a proud papa—he passed out cigars and sent out birth announce-

Jim Moran with his future son

ments. The national publicity that resulted more than compensated International Studios, the producers of *The Egg and I*, who paid Moran $2,000 for the stunt.

Variations on the egg-hatching concept have since been used successfully. In 1955, a Miami service station owner hoping to attract more customers paid a nubile blonde $300 to take a month off from her job as a waitress and attempt to hatch a nest of goose eggs. The young woman, attended by her own mother much of the time, sat in the station on the nest for twenty-eight days and finally hatched three goslings. This story actually appeared in the *New York Times*.

In 1969 the UPI wire services reported a story out of London in which a voluptuous newspaper reporter incubated a baby chick in her bosom. The woman was said to have tried the experiment after seeing a film made by Lord Snowdon in which a character in the film did the same thing. Actually, the stunt was enacted to promote the film. It took the woman twenty-one days to hatch the egg, and the new mother named her offspring Anthony Armstong-Jones.

WHALE WATCH

To promote the 1923 movie *Down to the Sea in Ships*, press agent Milton Crandall tipped Denver newspapers that a whale had been sighted on Pikes Peak. Crandall then raced up to the Peak and lay on his back shooting occasional sprays of seltzer into the air. According to newspaper accounts, hundreds of citizens gathered below pointing and shouting, "Thar she blows!"

A SICK STORY

Ringling Brothers Circus press agent Roland Butler frequently strained the credulity of reporters. Once the *Cincinnati Enquirer* printed a story which could not be verified. A circus giraffe, Butler's press release reported, had been arrested in Texas. It seems that the giraffe was prone to sore throats and required regular medications of bourbon, applied externally. Wherever it traveled, the circus carried along five cases of bourbon for the purpose. When the circus happened into a dry county in Texas, a vigilant lawman immediately impounded both giraffe and whiskey. It took the expert services of a high-priced lawyer to plead the case of the elongated sore throat.

Above, reporters on benches underwater wear aqualungs at the premiere of *Underwater*. The film's star, Jane Russell, here seen on the plastic screen, joined the reporters underwater. Below, the premiere of *Adam and Eve* required the original garb of the first man and woman. Preposterous premieres are a favorite ploy of film publicists.

Jack Benny turned to an outlandish idea to publicize a new season of his television show. His agency, Rogers and Cowan, sought a different angle to kick off what was in reality just another season. Henry Rogers, in his autobiography *Walking the Tightrope*, tells how the agency brainstormed: "Suddenly, an unfortunately long-forgotten associate held up his hand and timidly said, 'How about having Jack Benny host a party at the Automat.'"

The Automat was the cheapest place in New York to eat, hardly the usual haunt for the upscale show business crowd. But Benny had made a career out of being cheap—which made the tie-in perfect.

Invitations were sent out on penny postcards, which read:

> Over all the years I have had the reputation of being the cheapest man in Hollywood. I always resented this and have now decided to refute this unwarranted charge and prove that it isn't true.

As the guests arrived, Benny passed out rolls of nickels to each one and urged them to "have a good time."

Jack Benny played a violin duet with a chimpanzee while his guests selected items from the automat.

PUNS, PROVERBS, AND CLICHES

Preposterous language stunts taking off on puns, proverbs, and cliches might seem easy as pie to pull off but can be hard as a tack. It takes ingenuity to associate a client with a saying and one who takes the chance is liable to fall flat as a pancake.

Jim Moran, the press agent who challenged the maxim that you can't sell an icebox to an Eskimo, frequently thumbed through quotation books for an apt saying that he could turn into a stunt. Then he'd call a potential client and offer to stage the stunt on his or her behalf.

Rudy Vallee paid Moran $500 a week to determine how difficult it really was to find a needle in a haystack. The fee covered Moran's expenses and regular exclusive interviews on Vallee's radio show.

After an elaborate show of research to determine the average size of a haystack and the average size of a needle, Moran built a twelve-foot haystack in a Washington, D. C., parking lot and had a marked needle plunged into it. Dressed in a fitted aviator's suit, a miner's hat, goggles, and a dust respirator, Moran began the search. It took eighty-two hours to find the needle. All the while, crowds watched and newsreel cameras filmed. Periodically, Moran would break to be interviewed and to sell pieces of straw to the public at ten cents each. Each straw came in an envelope stamped with the following message:

Jim Moran, blindfolded for the search

MORAN NEEDLE-HUNTING EXPEDITION

This envelope contains one genuine bona fide straw from the Moran Haystack, situated on the corner of Connecticut Avenue and N Street, Northwest, in Washington, D.C., the Nation's Capital. This straw has been carefully inspected and closely scrutinized by Mr. Moran personally. He does aver, attest, affirm and pronounce this straw to be free and devoid of any needle whatsoever.
(Signed) Jim Moran

Satisfactorily answering the question about the needle in a haystack led Moran to wonder just how dangerous was a bull in a china shop. Orchestra leader Fred Waring, who had put Moran on retainer to ponder just such questions, was persuaded to research the problem by leading a bull into an exclusive china shop on New York City's 5th Avenue. While twelve reporters, twenty photographers, and seven newsreel crews stood by, Waring escorted a prize Jersey bull into the shop and let him loose. Nothing happened. The bull was placid as a cow, standing quietly as the flashbulbs popped. He didn't touch a single dish. In fact, the only damage was done by Waring himself, who, in his excitement, tripped and broke a couple of plates.

Moran later pulled off a different bovine stunt, this time on behalf of a New York dairy company. Rejecting "the cow jumped over the moon" as posing logistical problems, Moran racked his brain for cow-related sayings. When the verses "I never saw a purple cow, I never hope to see one" flashed through his mind, he realized he was onto something. At that time the song's writer, Gelett Burgess, lived in a hotel in New York. Moran obtained a cow from the dairy, mixed up some harmless purple dye, and painted her purple from head to tail. He also painted three of her teats gold and one silver and emblazoned the name of the dairy on her side. Then he went over to the hotel and rang up Burgess to come down to the lobby. A large group of reporters duly reported Burgess's astonishment.

During the 1944 presidential campaign, when the Democrats were declaring that you can't change horses in midstream, Moran was hired by the Republicans to prove otherwise. He went to Reno and waded out to the middle of the Truckee River, where he nimbly leaped from one horse to another. The photograph of Moran between horses was not enough to convince the country to change parties, and Roosevelt was re-elected by a wide margin.

Jim Moran,

changing horses in

midstream

Moran was not the only publicist to use proverbs for inspiration, although his stunts were among the most successful. Jet Fore, for years a publicist at Twentieth Century Fox, once had to publicize Robert Altman's movie *Health*. A scene in that movie featured characters at a health convention who dressed up like fruits and vegetables. "The picture was terrible," Fore recalled, "but I thought of the saying 'you can't get blood out of a turnip.'" He dressed a bunch of actors in turnip costumes and bussed them down to the local blood bank where they all donated a pint. Getting blood out of a turnip was easier than getting a story out of journalists in this case, but Fore swears the coverage was substantial.

In another test of cliches, the television show "Country Fair," popular in the fifties, wanted to test the adage "He can't punch his way out of a paper bag." For weeks various he-men of the day tried their luck inside a gigantic bag that was erected inside the studio. No one was successful but the attempts were the handle for news stories issued by the show's publicity department each week. Even *Sports Illustrated* devoted half a page to the story.

Chapter 5

Singing Dogs and Unemployed Parrots

Animal Stunts

Animals have been put to many uses, from plowing the field to decorating the sofa, but my favorite use for them has been to make them break through the front page as they would through a circus hoop.

Harry Reichenbach

Practically every furred and feathered creature in the menagerie, along with several species of marine animals, has been pressed into service by enterprising publicists. I've already touched on a few of these animal tales—the premiere for horses, the flight of Leo the Lion, the lion in T. R. Zann's hotel room, the purple cow, and the bull in the china shop. Here are a few more of my favorites.

ELEPHANT PILGRIMAGE

*A*nimals have always figured heavily in efforts to attract publicity. That's why it's illegal in North Carolina to plow a field with an elephant—it seems that P. T. Barnum pulled that stunt one too many times. He would position an elephant pulling a plow in a field next to the train tracks, believing that the odd sight would attract patrons to his circus. Apparently an irate farmer got tired of his field being torn up and advanced a bill in the state legislature.

Dexter Fellows, one of the singular breed of circus publicists whose ingenuity was seemingly endless, came up with an idea to promote the circus's 1922 New York City season. He decided to send a Ringling Brothers' elephant on a pilgrimage to lay a wreath on the grave of America's first elephant. This turned out to be one of those publicity stunts that make all who witness it smile.

Fellows arranged for Old John, a revered forty-year-old elephant, to walk the fifty-five miles from Madison Square Garden to Somers, New York, the site of the grave of and monument to Old Bet, the first elephant to be brought to the American continent. Old John was outfitted with leather boots to protect his feet from glass and nails on the long trek and draped with a banner stating his destination—and the fact that Ringling Brothers, Barnum and Bailey circus would be opening soon.

Reporters from the *New York Times*, the *Evening Post,* and the *New York World* rode behind the marching elephant in a convoy with Fellows. Inevitably, the stories they filed back had a whimsical tone. The *Evening Post* reported that, "Dexter Fellows, who knows his business, called up today to explain that in spite of advancing years Old John declined to 'travel light.' He insisted on carrying his trunk."

It took three days for the old pachyderm to reach his destination. All along the route, thousands of children came out to greet him. Then, as now, an elephant marching down the street was not a common sight, and each day, the journey was fully documented in all three papers. In Somers, an elaborate ceremony was held and thousands watched as Old John laid a wreath at the monument of Old Bet.

Dexter Fellows recalled what happened in his autobiography, *This Way to the Big Show.* "At the monument, gaily decorated with flags, another crowd was waiting . . . (who) took this matter of honoring Old Bet so seriously that, when the boys of the Lincoln Agricultural School sang the national anthem, it was hard to believe that the whole thing began as a publicity stunt. Perhaps it would be better to call it a journalistic holiday, for the stories written by the reporters assigned to the affair were little gems of humorous satire. It was only when I read them on the following day that my troubled conscience was put at rest, for I admit that I had no desire to exploit or make fun of this lovely rural community."

SOCIETY DEBUT

In the early twenties, Harry Reichenbach was hired to save the first *Tarzan of the Apes* movie from certain oblivion. The distributors' reaction to the preview had been uniformly negative and the filmmaker was about to see his life's savings go down the drain. But Reichenbach saw something in the film that others had not. He offered to take on the publicity of the film in exchange for a percentage of the box office receipts.

First he leased a theater and transformed it into an African jungle, complete with an authentic stuffed lion and live orangutans in cages swinging from coconut trees. Then he went to work on the stunt.

Just before the premiere the headlines appeared: "SIMIAN ROYALTY STEPS OUT" and "JUNGLE PRINCE MAKES SOCIETY DEBUT." Reichenbach had struck again. He had dressed an orangutan in a tuxedo and high hat and taken it to the exclusive Knickerbocker Hotel, where society mingled on Saturday nights. The well-dressed simian spun through the revolving door and greeted the assembly with a jungle call.

When the pandemonium died down, the orangutan had been hauled off to jail and *Tarzan of the Apes* was on its way to becoming a hit movie. In recalling the incident years later, Reichenbach said, "The idea that it would be possible for a monkey dressed in natty clothes to crash into society was something unusual, unbelievable, and when it happened, it furnished front-page material. The fact that I had planted this episode and used it to promote the Tarzan picture, established more firmly in my mind that the whole difference between the things that are dreamed about and reality was simply a matter of projection."

The Paramount publicity department trained fifty parrots to repeat "It Ain't No Sin," the title of a forthcoming Mae West movie. This required an intensive effort over many weeks. The parrots were kept in a room at the studio and a professional bird trainer was brought in to rehearse the flock. Reporters were invited to come by and see the birds and hear their progress first hand. The idea was to stock each of fifty theaters with one trained parrot to attract publicity in all the major markets. Just days before the movie was released, disaster struck—or so the press releases said. The producers capriciously changed the title of the film to *I'm No Angel*. There wasn't time to retrain the parrots, so the publicists called a press conference and said they were releasing them back into the jungle. Many newspaper stories recounted the "mishap," while slipping in information about the forthcoming film—under its correct title, of course.

Jim Moran was hired by the manufacturers of a product called X-M, which was supposed to keep eyeglasses from fogging. The makers were sure that if they could just get their product mentioned in the news, there would be a large market for it. Moran turned to pigeons for help. He rounded up a hundred homing pigeons from a breeder in New York and took them to Washington, D.C., where he outfitted each with a tiny pair of spectacles.

The newspapers and wire service reporters were then summoned to his hotel to witness research in action. The spectacles of half the pigeons were treated with X-M (and clearly marked with the initials); the specs of the other birds were left untreated. The premise to be tested, Moran proclaimed, was that the pigeons with the X-M would arrive back in New York first owing to the product's defogging abilities. All the news stories focused on the beginning of the flight, with photographs of the pigeons prominently featuring the client's name. By the end of the race, the press had lost interest, though Moran later claimed that the hypothesis had been borne out.

A bank in Basel, Switzerland, attempted to attract publicity to its move to new headquarters by using camels for the operation. At first all went well.

Then the weight shifted on one camel's load and the animal bolted, dragging a bank official with him. No one was hurt, but press agents sometimes learn the hard way that animals can be unpredictable.

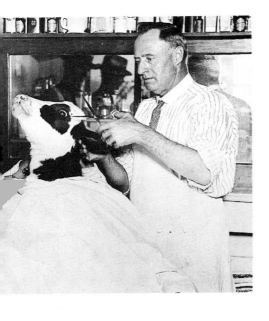

A cow gets a trim in an Oakland, California, barber shop promotion.

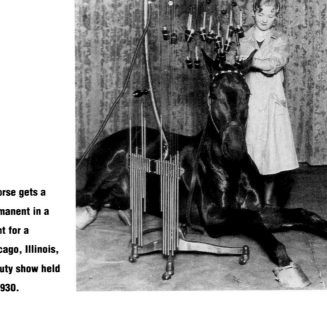

A horse gets a permanent in a stunt for a Chicago, Illinois, beauty show held in 1930.

Bubbles the elephant water skis to promote the movie *Honky Tonk Freeway*.

In New York City's Gimbels sixth-floor toy department, Beaulah the calf and Magnolia her nursemaid cow get ready for Christmas.

An early spokesdog takes to the streets to promote the name change of his employer, Uneeda Biscuit.

Animals were the preferred stars of many of the stunts rigged by Ringling Brothers, Barnum and Bailey veteran press agent Roland Butler. Once when the circus was wintering in Sarasota, Florida, an aged lion named Brutus was approaching his final days. An accident while eating had resulted in a fractured jawbone and several broken teeth. Unless the damage was repaired, Brutus would not survive.

Butler decided to stage a public operation and invite the press. Although surgery on animals is now commonplace, in Butler's day it was highly unusual. The prospect of a man sticking his hand into a lion's mouth added additional human interest.

Butler had a clinic set up in a clean cage and outfitted the veterinarian in a white smock and a hat with a surgeon's mirror. While the media watched, Brutus was injected with ether. As soon as he was asleep, the vet wired his jaw and inserted two false teeth.

The operation over, Butler invited the press to return the following day to see the patient. Unfortunately, Brutus never revived; he had been too old to withstand the anesthesia. This did not faze Butler, however. When the newsmen arrived, they found a frisky lion chomping on a bone in Brutus's cage. The press agent had substituted a healthy middle-aged male for the deceased and no one spotted the difference.

The success of the operation was duly recorded in the local papers and Butler viewed the clippings with great satisfaction. "It's contributions of this sort that make circus publicity an extremely valuable science," he told *The New Yorker* magazine.

BAND-AID SOLUTION

Jet Fore, working for Marine World in Los Angeles, once got national coverage on a stunt featuring an enormous killer whale. It seems that the theme park's whale had been swimming too close to the side of the tank and had scraped his skin. Fore contacted a bandage company and arranged for a gigantic bandage to be made for the whale. Divers had a difficult time affixing it, but the sight of them trying was comical and the crowds at the whale shows swelled.

Starlet Linda Hutchins dressed in a nurse's costume to change the band-aid on Bubbles the Whale.

A search for the nation's best singing dog was the perfect stunt to launch a new dog food, called Solo. Playing on the idea of "O Solo Mio," the manufacturer, Wayne Pet Foods, set up a series of regional contests that corresponded with the introduction of Solo in the various marketing areas. "What we're looking for," a company spokesman said, "is a singing dog who fits the Wayne image of quality. If we find one, we may naturally want to use him to help get our message across."

The regional competitions were hotly contested. In Chicago, for example, some fifty hopefuls participated. Wayne was able to parlay the contests into a national story that made the front page of the *Wall Street Journal*. It was not the last time that corporate America would use an animal "spokesperson" with great success.

Spuds MacKenzie, "spokesparty animal" for Bud Light, is an example of how an animal has been used not just in a one-time publicity stunt, but as a total marketing phenomenon. This eighties superstar has generated millions of dollars worth of free publicity for his sponsor.

Spuds, who bears an uncanny resemblance to an English Bull Terrier (the people with Bud Light won't admit he's a dog), began his commercial career in 1983, when DDB Needham, a Chicago ad agency, put his image on a Bud Light poster targeting beer drinkers aged twenty-one to thirty-four. His comical appearance with his black eye patch and pointy ears made him a cult figure on college campuses, and Anheuser-Busch decided to make him a key figure in Bud Light's national advertising campaign. Television commercials featuring Spuds as the "Original Party Animal" led to a blitz of merchandising spin-offs, from posters to department store "Spuds boutiques." In addition, Spuds makes personal appearances all over the country. During halftime at football games, Spuds and his retinue of beautiful women (the

Spudettes) arrive on the playing field regally waving to the crowd from convertible limousines. Spuds looka-like contests have attracted hundreds of contestants—both dogs and humans—and Spuds impostors have secured lucrative modeling contracts. Spuds himself has been pursued for several movie roles and even has a staff of three to handle his fan mail.

Spuds is that happy idea that became a national fad—and he has worked well selling the product he represents. Sales of Bud Light increased approximately 20 percent in 1986, 1987, and 1988. Although the mania over Spuds merchandise has quieted, his commercials for Bud Light continue to be among the most popular on television.

The party animal himself, surrounded by loyal followers

Chapter 6

Photo Opportunity

Planned Posings

> My idea of a good picture is one of a famous person doing something infamous. It's being in the right place at the wrong time.
> Andy Warhol

When a press release arrives on an editor's desk, it gets special attention if it's marked "photo opportunity." This phrase tells the editor that the press agent will be creating a situation that will make an interesting photo. Props, costumes, an unusual location, a good-looking woman, a young child, or a celebrity are all variables used to enhance the photogenic potential. Editors are always on the lookout for a good photo opportunity and will sometimes cover a story for the photo alone.

The technology to reproduce photographs in newspapers was not perfected until the end of the nineteenth century. The *New York Tribune* published the first photo on January 21, 1897, but it wasn't until 1910 that photos became standard in most U.S. newspapers. The *Illustrated Daily News*, which featured a huge front-page photo and back-page photos of beauty contestants, was founded in 1919 and was the first of a number of photo newspapers that flourished throughout the twenties. Faked photos, made of several pictures pasted together, were a staple of these scandal sheets.

Today, a handful of newspapers will only print photographs taken by their staff photographers, but most print media are avid consumers of photographs that will illustrate their stories or that might serve as stories in themselves. It's standard practice to print photographs submitted by press agents, and the wire services will often pick up a good photo from such outside sources and send it to thousands of newspapers around the country. But whatever its source, a good news photo reflects a certain kind of cooperation between subject and photographer. We think of news photos as spontaneous, lucky shots, but many are as carefully orchestrated as an advertising photo. This section features a sample of the century's most creative and amusing staged photos.

This classic photo was staged to promote *The Seven Year Itch*. Special windblowers were installed in the grate below Monroe's feet and photographers were summoned to capture her skirt as it "accidentally" flew up.

A bathing beauty contest in 1952 features Bonzo the Chimpanzee, then an international movie star in his own right. The contest was designed to bring attention to the up-and-coming starlet Anita Ekberg.

Greta Garbo disdainfully cooperates in an early studio publicity stunt.

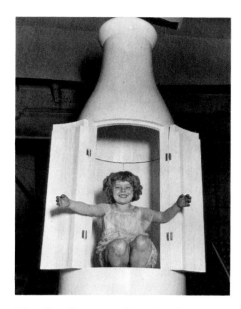

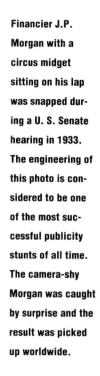

A long-forgotten dairy built this milk bottle prop to enhance the photo opportunity

Financier J.P. Morgan with a circus midget sitting on his lap was snapped during a U. S. Senate hearing in 1933. The engineering of this photo is considered to be one of the most successful publicity stunts of all time. The camera-shy Morgan was caught by surprise and the result was picked up worldwide.

Child star Jackie Coogan immortalizes his hand prints at the Grauman's Chinese Theater.

Baby kissing and nuzzling is a sure-fire image builder —whether the baby likes it or not. Over the years public figures, especially politicians, have come to rely upon a few tried and true photo set-ups, like these. From top left, clockwise: Harry Truman, Pope John Paul II, Lyndon Johnson, Richard Nixon, Jesse Jackson, George Bush

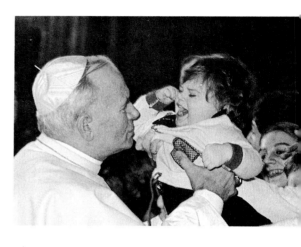

Put on a hat and call in the photographers. From top left, clockwise: Harry Truman, Richard Nixon, Gerald Ford, Michael Dukakis, George Bush, Ronald Reagan

John Lennon and Yoko Ono understood the value of an unusual set-up to attract publicity. Here, they are photographed during their famous bed-in, held on their honeymoon in 1969 to focus attention on their concern for world peace.

Retail mogul Sam Walton hulas down Wall Street, as he promised his WalMart employees he would do if profits went up. His prominence and his attire guaranteed a wire service photo.

A dummy of Alfred Hitchcock floats down the Thames River during the shooting of the movie *Frenzy*. Hitchcock was a master of publicity and liked to use his own image whenever possible.

Chapter 7

It's a Long Story
Shaggy Dog Stunts

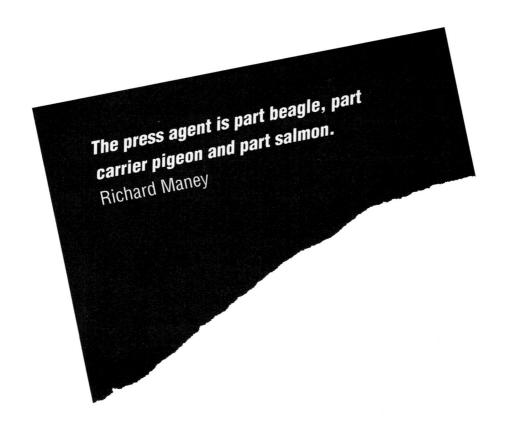

The press agent is part beagle, part carrier pigeon and part salmon.

Richard Maney

Many stunts require a convoluted buildup to be effective; an elaborate story must first be told for the stunt to "work." I call these "shaggy dog" or "it's-a-long-story" stunts. Not many of this type are seen today—these stunts really flourished in the heyday of print.

A SHORT CUT

A man got into a cab in New York City, asked the driver to take him to Juarez, and promptly fell asleep. The cabby woke him in Philadelphia demanding gas money. "What are we doing in Philadelphia?" the passenger screamed. "It's the quickest route to Mexico," the cabby replied. "You idiot, I meant the movie *Juarez*," the passenger hollered. The passenger, of course, then refused to pay and the two proceeded to the nearest police station to report each other's stupidity. This story was picked up by all the local newspapers and no one realized that both the cabby and the passenger were in the studio employ.

SIGNED, STUART LITTLE

In the 1940s newspapers around the country began receiving letters to the editor signed by a Stuart Little. Stating that he was a researcher on crows, Little asked for help in verifying the lifespan of a crow. He challenged the government statistics that the average crow lived only for twelve years. Little said that he was certain that some of the estimated 3 billion crows in America lived longer. He asked readers to send authenticated reports of old crows to him. Thousands of readers responded and it seemed for a time that everyone was talking about old crows. This was just what Little had hoped for. Needless to say, his client, Old Crow Bourbon, was pleased with the results.

While attending an American Legion convention in New York City, a Boston barkeep named Diogenes Pelichronos found a bracelet in Times Square. It was inscribed, "Please return to Sandra Carpenter, 1547 Broadway." The address was that of a theater where a new movie, *Lured*, was being premiered. And it soon turned out that the leading character in the film was named Sandra Carpenter. When Diogenes arrived to return the bracelet, a group of reporters, summoned by the movie's press agent, were waiting to interview him. Much was made of the coincidence that a man named Diogenes had found the bracelet and turned it in— his namesake the ancient Greek Diogenes devoted his life to searching for an honest man. What the reporters never knew was that Diogenes himself was a plant. When the press agents had learned that the film premiere would coincide with the American Legion convention, they had pored over the membership roster looking for a name to involve in the stunt. Originally, Pelichronos had no intention of attending the convention, but the studio paid for him to fly to New York and attend just so a Diogenes could find the bracelet. Talk about convoluted!

It is generally agreed that critics' reviews make or break a Broadway play, so it was understandable that producer David Merrick would be upset when his 1962 debut of *Subways Are for Sleeping* was panned by all seven of New York's top critics. But Merrick, who had a flair for publicity, decided to retaliate.

In the New York phone directories, he found seven names identical to those of the leading critics. Merrick called these men and invited them to see the show as his guest. Afterwards he treated them to a lavish meal and party. In exchange he asked to use their names and photographs in an upcoming promotion. All agreed, and Merrick and his press agents then wrote and produced an ad with this headline: "SEVEN OUT OF SEVEN ARE ECSTATICALLY UNANIMOUS ABOUT *SUBWAYS ARE FOR SLEEPING*." The ad featured photos of Merrick's seven citizens and their enthusiastic comments about the play.

At that time, Howard Taubman was the drama critic for the *New York Times*. In his review he had written, "The play's book is dull and vapid and its characters barely breathe." Merrick's Howard Taubman declared, "One of the few great musical comedies of the last thirty years, one of the best of our time."

The *Tribune*'s Walter Kerr had actually written that the play was a "noble try," which moved "as fitfully as the holiday traffic." Merrick's Kerr enthused, "What a show. What a hit. What a solid hit!"

Merrick tried to place the ad in all seven newspapers but was foiled by alert advertising managers in six of them. The *New York Herald Tribune* ran the ad in its first edition but then pulled it in subsequent editions. Still, the attempt was enough to generate stories in all seven newspapers, and the show got a fresh round of publicity as a result.

When the Better Business Bureau of New York got wind of the caper, it sharply criticized Merrick and asked that he refrain from using the ad in any public medium, such as placards or mail circulars. But Merrick was far from penitent. "Broadway needed something to laugh about," he declared.

PLAY ON WORDS

Richard Maney was one of the most successful Broadway press agents and in his day handled as many plays at any one time as the union allowed. He had a particular flair with a press release, and newspapers would often print his writings verbatim. "The press agent is part beagle, part carrier pigeon and part salmon," he once said. When asked to explain he said, "the salmon goes home to die." He once pulled off a shaggy dog stunt when he ran an ad on behalf of a Broadway bomb *The Squall*. It read, "See the play that made a streetwalker of Robert Benchley." Benchley, a reviewer for *The New Yorker* at the time, had been less than impressed by the play. *The Squall* featured a gypsy waif named Nubi who spoke in pidgin English. At one point she says, "Nubi good girl. Nubi stay?" Benchley, in his review replied, "Benchley bad boy, Benchley go." Maney's "streetwalker ads" were rejected by all papers until he changed "streetwalker" to "nocturnal nomad." The story tickled the columnists and the resulting publicity led to an eight-month extension of *The Squall*'s run.

Jim Moran, who excelled at the shaggy dog stunt, was hired by Pimm's Cup, an English gin drink, to come up with a stunt that would entice the world into trying this new alcoholic beverage. Moran came up with a complicated scheme that was really a minidrama. Two couples (all well-known actors of the day) were enlisted to go to a trendy New York nightclub and to order Pimm's Cup. One couple arrived first and was nursing Pimm's Cups when the second couple entered and sat nearby. The second woman loudly ordered a Pimm's Cup with a sprig of mint. The first couple loudly objected, claiming that Pimm's Cup was to be served with cucumber rind, not mint. Soon the argument had escalated into a full-scale fight—tables were overturned and punches thrown. The four ended up in jail, to be duly bailed out by Jim Moran. The story made the front page of the *World Telegram* and the third page of the *Sun*, and a number of columns were written debating the virtues of mint over cucumber rind in a Pimm's Cup. The best part of the stunt, from the client's point of view, was that the story could not be told without mentioning Pimm's Cup.

In the early twenties, Harry Reichenbach once staged an elaborate campaign to publicize a silent movie. At the time, a group called the Lord's Day Alliance was trying to get national legislation passed that would outlaw entertainment on Sundays. Suddenly, billboards around the country were plastered with ominous warnings:

IF YOU DANCE ON SUNDAY, YOU ARE OUTSIDE THE LAW.

IF YOU MOTOR ON SUNDAY, YOU ARE OUTSIDE THE LAW.

IF YOU PLAY GOLF ON SUNDAY, YOU ARE OUTSIDE THE LAW.

IF YOU PLAY POOL ON SUNDAY, YOU ARE OUTSIDE THE LAW.

In the corner of each poster was an official-looking shield bearing the initials P. D. No one knew who was behind the billboards, and there was much speculation in the newspapers. The assumption was that P. D. stood for Police Department, but law officials denied any connection with the campaign. People in the entertainment industry became quite concerned that some type of censorship was imminent. Soon Universal Films announced that it would respond to these posters with a series of its own. The studio's first billboard read:

**IGNORE MALICIOUS
PROGAGANDA!**

**YOU ARE NOT
OUTSIDE THE LAW
IF YOU DANCE ON SUNDAY.**

There followed a series of similar announcements. All were marked with the shield bearing the letters P. D. The elaborate buildup went on for many weeks before the reason behind it finally became clear. Universal Films announced a forthcoming movie, *Outside the Law*. Although it had nothing to do with censorship, Harry Reichenbach hadn't been able to resist tying it in with the local news, especially when he realized that the star, Priscilla Dean, had the perfect initials for carrying out the stunt. The police department was upset by this blatant attempt to involve it in a hoax, but did not arrest anyone. After all, nothing about the stunt was actually . . . outside the law.

Chapter 8

Creating the Seal of Approval

Polls, Surveys, and Expert Opinions

I would to God, thou and I knew where a commodity of good names were to be bought.

Falstaff

A favorite strategy of the public relations practitioner and press agent alike is to stamp a stunt with an expert's seal of approval. A psychologist's opinion, a "scientific" poll or survey, an intricate machine that measures a reaction—all these are ploys used to corroborate or legitimatize the newsworthiness of the publicist's presentation.

NUTS!

After consulting with concessionaires, circus press agent Roland Butler once released a "scientific" survey of peanut eating by spectators at the circus. He reported that after sixty-five performances the public had consumed exactly 27,741,000 peanuts, a number considerably greater, he asserted, than that of the previous year. This proved that the current show was the most thrilling in Ringling's history, Butler concluded. Reporters were perplexed by his logic. "It's reflected in the peanut eating," Butler informed them. "When the acts are dangerous, people eat peanuts out of nervousness. They've been eating them by the ton."

THE LOVE TEST

Who are the most passionate—blondes, brunettes, or redheads? This age-old debate was once settled scientifically by the publicity department of MGM. In 1927, a novice press agent, Hubert Voight, was assigned the New York publicity for the upcoming film *Love*, starring Greta Garbo.

Love featured many passionate scenes between Garbo and John Gilbert, and Voight decided to use these scenes in a "psychological" experiment. He enlisted the help of a psychologist from Columbia University who agreed to test blondes, brunettes, and redheads for their response to the *Love* scenes. The women would be hooked up to a machine (an early, crude version of the lie detector), which would measure their blood pressure and respiration rates. The most responsive would be declared the most passionate.

Nine beautiful showgirls—three blondes, three brunettes, and three redheads—were recruited from the Zeigfield Follies to participate in the experiment. Voight sent out press releases on purloined Columbia University stationery and attracted a small army of reporters and photographers on the given day.

First the psychologist gave a grave and scholarly presentation about the nature of passion. Then each woman in turn was hooked up and her responses were recorded. To no one's surprise, the brunettes were the clear winners. According to writer Larry Engelman, who interviewed Voight sixty years later, "Patsy O'Day and Peggy Udell, the brunettes, showed truly gratifying excitement in seeing the love scenes on the big screen. They squirmed and blushed and became visibly agitated. The redheads wriggled a bit but not so convincingly. And the blondes just sat there, bored and impatient. One blonde, in fact, had to cut short her part in the experiment to hurry home and, she said, cook dinner for her mother."

The experiment, dubbed "The Love Test" in the many stories that subsequently went out across the country, had a twofold benefit in proving that brunettes are most passionate. First, it confirmed the love potential of Greta Garbo, a brunette. Second, it challenged a rival picture of the day, *Gentlemen Prefer Blondes*. The experiment was rigged, of course, but no one demanded a retest.

Facsimile from the original press release that announced the results of the "love test"

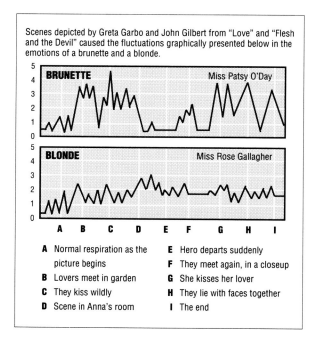

Scenes depicted by Greta Garbo and John Gilbert from "Love" and "Flesh and the Devil" caused the fluctuations graphically presented below in the emotions of a brunette and a blonde.

BRUNETTE — Miss Patsy O'Day

BLONDE — Miss Rose Gallagher

A   B   C   D   E   F   G   H   I

A Normal respiration as the picture begins
B Lovers meet in garden
C They kiss wildly
D Scene in Anna's room
E Hero departs suddenly
F They meet again, in a closeup
G She kisses her lover
H They lie with faces together
I The end

HAT HYPE

Russell Birdwell was once hired by the dying hat industry to try to rejuvenate it. People were just not wearing hats in the numbers they had been. Men in particular were abandoning head covers in record numbers. Birdwell wondered whether there might be a psychological reason for this defection. He arranged for a psychologist at Texas University to be commissioned to study the problem. The doctor soon came up with a diagnosis: men who go bareheaded, it was announced, revealed feminine instincts. This was in the 1940s when the concern about such things was more acute than it is today.

Columnists debated the manliness of wearing a hat. Princeton men, who had stopped wearing hats in 1904, were exhorted to resume. "Masculine" types, such as John Wayne, were photographed wearing hats. This was just one strategy in Birdwell's overall campaign. Another of his schemes involved convincing women to wear men's straw hats. Ultimately, Birdwell's combined efforts resulted in a 30 percent rise in hat sales. One company reported a profit of $1,200,000 after having lost twice that amount the previous year.

Alas, the hat industry failed to sustain its success. A decade later executives had to turn again to press agentry. This time they hired Guido Orlando to help stimulate their flagging sales. Orlando took a tack similar to Birdwell's. He formed an organization called The Religious Institute of Research and had it conduct a survey of hat wearers. The survey revealed that more than 22 million Roman Catholic women were going to church bareheaded, and these results were publicized nationwide. Orlando, a native Italian who had emigrated to America as a boy, still had strong connections in his homeland. In an impressive show of the strength of his connections, he was able to get the Pope himself to decree that women's heads must be covered in church. Once again hat sales soared.

Staged photo promoting a new line of hats

Jim Moran designed and built with his own hands a machine to test the happiness of women. Called a hapometer, it consisted of a small box with a complex display of dials and quivering needles. Armed with this contraption, Moran set out on a twenty-city tour to find the woman who would be crowned "Miss Happy as a Lark."

The elaborate stunt was designed to promote Lark automobiles, manufactured by Studebaker, whose dealers participated nationwide. The winner was to receive a Lark convertible. Contestants were hooked up to the hapometer and asked such questions as "How's your love life?" and "Do you drink much?" Moran would then pronounce the results.

In each city, Moran managed to get a story in the local newspaper, and the client's name would always be mentioned prominently. He was foiled in Minneapolis, however, where a reporter for the *Tribune* wrote a clever article naming just about every automobile then being manufactured except the Lark:

**Jim Moran
conducting his
happiness test**

122

Jim Moran is a world-renowned rambler.

In his many travels as a press agent, he has been known to ford a river or brave localities where the mercury knows no bounds in order to plant a sponsor's name.

Moran is well known in Cadillac and Pontiac, Mich. and in the imperial palaces of the Orient. On the other hand, he has never been in Buyck or Austin, Minn.

He has pulled many a dodge, but in general he is known in the trade as being solid as Plymouth Rock.

Moran has a beard like Lincoln that gives many people the willies. He is built in somewhat Goliath proportions and has the eye of an explorer, like DeSoto.

Moran was in Minneapolis promoting a contest to find "The Happiest Girl in America." The winner will receive a screen test and a new automobile, the maker of which is his sponsor.

However, it didn't take long for Moran to turn this into even more coverage for his client—*Time* magazine was so amused by the article that it reproduced it in its entirety along with a story on the Lark promotion.

KISSES AND CREEPS AT THE MOVIES

Marty Weiser was promoting *Lassiter*, a nondescript movie starring Tom Selleck, for Warner Brothers. The movie was scheduled for release on Valentine's Day, which set Weiser to thinking about a kissing contest. "Tom Selleck was and is loved by most women," Weiser recalled. "You talk to most women and they say, 'Oh Tom Selleck—would I like to meet him.'" Weiser couldn't get Selleck to appear in person, so he opted for the next best thing. He had a fourteen-foot blowup made of the star's face and announced that the studio was on the search for "the girl with the kissable lips."

A great big kisser

About a week before the event, an executive at Warner Brothers tried to get Weiser to cancel the stunt. He said "Nobody's going to kiss a photo—no way. You're nuts. It won't work. No one is going to show up." "I almost cancelled," Weiser recalled, "But I decided that I believed in it and that I was going to try it."

Contestants were to kiss the photograph of Selleck with red lipstick and leave an imprint that an "expert" would then evaluate. This expert, an official-looking individual, studied each imprint with a magnifying glass and determined from "the heat of it, the position on the photo, and the clarity of the imprint, who were the winners." Actually, there were many winners, and they all got to see the first show for free.

As usual Weiser had been right. More than three hundred women had shown up anxious and ready to plant a kiss on Selleck's face. "As a matter of fact, seven TV stations showed up and all of the women reporters also kissed the picture." Weiser had the instinct for what would sell a movie no matter how goofy the idea seemed around a conference table.

For another film, *Creep Show*, Weiser devised a special device, "a creep detector," based on the airport metal detectors, to test the authenticity of creeps. Then he offered free admittance to people who arrived at the theater dressed as creeps and who made it through the sensing device. The detector broadcast a weird assortment of sounds in response to each creep who entered the booth, and, as reporters scribbled, Hollywood played host to one more lineup of people in costume, patiently waiting their turns. Hopefuls who were insufficiently creepy were rejected by the creep detector, whose criteria for judgment remained unchallenged, and had to pay for their tickets.

Weiser's machine uncovering a real creep

Chapter 9

Competition Fever

Contests, Races, and Records

In every field of human endeavor, he that is first must perpetually live in the white light of publicity.

Theodore F. MacManus,
Saturday Evening Post, January 2, 1915

Contests take many forms. In some, the public can enter for a monetary or prize reward; others are contests of strength, beauty, talent, skill, or endurance in which individuals compete primarily to be proclaimed the best. A contest dreamed up by a public relations person practically guarantees success at hooking publicity for the client as long as the contest itself is clever or the prize is significant.

P. T. Barnum is credited by some sources with conducting the first recorded contest in the United States. In 1850 he offered a $200 prize for the best song written about the "Swedish Nightingale," Jenny Lind. Hundreds of people entered and the winning lyrics were duly published in all the papers of the day. This was part of an avalanche of promotion Barnum planned when he brought the songstress from Europe to tour this country.

Barnum's rival, the appropriately named circus owner Adam Forepaugh, staged a contest on a much bigger scale: "The $10,000 Beauty Contest." Ten thousand dollars was an enormous amount of money in the mid-nineteenth century and many young women vied for the title. The winner, Louise Montague, was declared the most beautiful woman in

the world. But the contest itself was rigged. Montague was paid $100 a week as a circus employee and never saw the $10,000. Nevertheless, she led the big Forepaugh street parades into each city, and huge crowds gathered to get a firsthand look at the "winner." Forepaugh's circus receipts doubled after the contest.

Louise Montague

As the profession matured, contests became a staple in the PR industry's cupboard; thousands of contests are created every year by PR practitioners as a surefire way of guaranteeing coverage. Some, such as the Ivory Soap carving contests sponsored by Procter and Gamble, are germane to the client's product, and some are simply wacky ideas that attract attention for their sheer zaniness and the willingness of people to actually participate.

The best are not only reliable publicity getters but sociological curiosities in their own right. Too many have been launched over the years to be included in this brief survey, but a few of the especially notable are celebrated here.

The queen of "National Hot Dog Week" was selected by employees of the Zion Meat Products Company, (right); a queen of "National Cranberry Week" promotes the fruit (below). Beauty queen contests are excellent vehicles for publicizing products or industries.

VALENTINE'S MANUAL

BARNUM'S MUSEUM
Every Day and Evening this Week, commencing Monday, June 2nd, 1862

GRAND NATIONAL

Waters & Son

BABY SHOW
100 BEAUTIFUL BABIES
will be on exhibition for prizes, for which upwards of
$2,000 Cash will be Distributed
FOR THE
Finest Babies,
Twins, Triplets,
Quaterns.
—AND—
ANOTHER BARNUM'S MUSEUM ATTRACTION. 1862

P. T. Barnum staged beautiful-baby contests to attract patrons to his museum.

SEVEN IN ONE BLOW

Certainly one of the more unusual public relations campaigns was launched by various public health organizations in the early 1900s to eradicate the common housefly. Scientific studies of the day seemed to prove that the fly transmitted infectious disease, and it was decided that the media be used in an attempt to get rid of the pest. "Swat the Fly" contests were mounted in cities across the nation in which boys and girls were awarded prizes based on the number of flies they killed.

In Washington, D. C., more than five thousand children participated in a two-week-long slaughter. Sponsored by the *Washington Evening Star*, the contest's top prize for the most flies killed was $25. The body count was conducted by the city health department, which asserted that more than seven million flies had been flattened. The first-prize winner, a thirteen-year-old boy named Layton H. Burdette, was credited with a stupendous 343,800 kill. The young entrepreneur had formed a company of twenty-five children to collect the bounty and split the prize money.

In other parts of the country, school principals selected grammar school children as "Junior Sanitary Police." The catches of these squads were tabulated and honors for top body counts were publicized. The national antifly campaign petered out around 1915, either because the number of flies had actually decreased through these efforts or the menace seemed diminished by the ensuing world war.

Boy scouts participate in a health department public relations blitz. This one was an antispitting campaign.

It was none other than public relations "father" Edward Bernays who persuaded Procter and Gamble to launch the first nationwide Ivory Soap carving competition in 1924. The company set up the "National Soap Sculpture Committee" to conduct the contest. No one realized that first year that a national phenomenon had been launched that would play an important part in the childhoods of generations of Americans.

Early participants were mostly professional artists and adults, and many sculptures were carved out of five-hundred and thousand-pound blocks of soap. The larger the piece, the greater was the publicity value. From the beginning Procter and Gamble paid for a promotional staff that lathered every possible publicity angle from the contest.

Winning pieces or photographs of them were routed more or less throughout the country, with suitable attention being given to soap sculpture and Ivory Soap. As the years went by the number of entries increased from a few hundred to thousands. Gradually the categories were changed to phase out adults and to allow children only to enter in three age groups.

Each year between the announcement of the contest and the close of the competition, the promotional staff labored full time to maintain interest. Special pieces of enormous size were commissioned and exhibited. In the twenties and thirties life-sized sculptures of current heroes such as Charles Lindbergh were toured. Over the years entries included a complete set of chessmen, a forty-piece orchestra, a nativity scene, the Empire State Building carved according to the original blueprints, many historic temples and buildings, a medieval battle scene, and famous football scenes in action.

Window display promoting soap sculpture

130

Photographs of entries were printed in virtually every newspaper in America, while how-to-carve articles and related human interest stories were seemingly endless. In the thirties, Procter and Gamble rented the sixty-fifth floor of Rockefeller Center as a place to exhibit the entries. In the first month, there were fifty thousand visitors to the exhibition.

One hiatus in the relentless promotion of soap sculpture occurred when a New York City soap carver took a turn at practicing his art on a young woman and her mother. Hiding in the home of his victims while they were out, he gathered a number of cakes of soap from around the house and started carving, and by the time the women returned home he had finished a number of pieces. He then killed both and fled the scene of the crime, leaving the bodies and the completed soap sculptures. Police brought in Henry Bern, the public relations counsel for the contest, who after many years of judging contests was an expert on carving style. He instantly recognized the work of a previous year's prize winner.

Prize winning soap sculpture, a facsimile of the original Macy's department store

In a letter to Procter and Gamble years later, Bern reminisced:

I realized I had to do some quick thinking . . . never easy for me and under these circumstances doubly hard because it was quite some time since I was associated with gruesome murder—but something had to be said and it had to be said fast. I disclaimed knowing the murderer, criticized the pieces as very amateurish and doubted that they were the works of an adult, stating further they had all the earmarks of being the work of young girls. A reporter present was very disappointed and so expressed himself. In fact he suggested if I could change my opinions both Soap Sculpture and I could get a lot of publicity. I told him no one was sorrier than I that the facts are as I stated them, and it would be folly to say otherwise, because there are thousands of people who could and would contradict false statements.

Bern's quick thinking kept soap sculpture free of this unfortunate association, and although the murderer was quickly apprehended and convicted, never a word appeared in the newspapers about the link between the murders and Procter and Gamble. Thus, the contest continued, unsullied, until the early sixties when interest finally began to decline. Procter and Gamble recently fanned the spirit of the contest again by commissioning sculptor Gary L. Sussman to carve a statue of a six-foot-tall forty-niner gold miner, as an "art educational project" for the people of San Francisco. Whacking away at a six-thousand pound bar of Ivory Soap, the sculptor was hoping to qualify for a place in the *Guinness Book of World Records* with the largest permanent soap sculpture.

Meanwhile a hundred San Francisco school children were taken on a field trip to Union Square to learn about the "folk art" of soap carving. They were provided with little bars of Ivory Soap and plastic knives to carve with. The event was widely covered in the San Francisco media demonstrating once again that old publicity stunts never die—at least not before they're squeezed and squeezed to the last sliver.

SITTING IN SUBSTANCES

A radio station in Boise, Idaho, had a jumping-in-Jell-O contest. Prizes were awarded for the largest numbers of marbles retrieved from the bottom of a 4.5-foot deep, 600-gallon tank filled with gooey green Jell-O. More than one thousand spectators watched.

This was a variation on a category of contests I call "sitting in substances." In contests of endurance, people have immersed themselves in vanilla pudding, chicken soup, spaghetti, and most recently, baked beans with hotdogs. This last took place in San Francisco. To bring attention to the plight of AIDS victims, a man spent twenty-four hours neck-high in a bathtub filled with beans.

Disk jockey Tom Nicolson goes for the first world record in spaghetti sitting in a contest sponsored by radio station WLAM in Auburn, Maine.

BIG MOUTH

To promote the movie *Jaws II*, the Plitt Theaters in Century City held a search for the largest set of jaws in Los Angeles. Their public relations firm set up an eating contest in which the bites of contestants were measured and the largest was deemed winner. In fact, the agency, Ruder and Finn, piggybacked another of its clients, Nabisco, onto the effort by using a huge Fig Newton as the chomping medium.

NICE WORK IF YOU CAN GET IT

A 1988 "Couch Potato" contest attracted unexpected notoriety for Sonoma County, California, and proved to be a harvest of publicity for the county fair. Vying for the title of "Designated Couch Potato," contestants had to demonstrate why they qualified as most sluggish of all. The prize was a two-week job at the fair at a total salary of $1,000. The job description consisted of eating and watching TV on a couch in an exhibit.

A controversy erupted when health food enthusiasts objected to the whole idea of the contest, saying it would set a bad example to children. Their protests intimidated the fair officials into selecting as winner a man whom other contestants claimed was far from meeting the requirements. The winner, a twenty-four-year-old student named John Silveira was beefy at 210 pounds, that was true, but he also was a known hiker and bicyclist. A true couch potato's only exercise is pressing the remote control button of the television set. Not only that but Silveira had been observed eating yogurt and once was overheard discussing a public television program.

The runner-up, a three-hundred-pound unemployed maintenance man, was outraged at the injustice. His credentials—regular consumption of Cheez-its and Ding Dongs smothered with jam and around-the-clock watching of sitcoms and quiz shows on television—surely made him the clear winner. The story received national coverage with most observers siding with the runner-up. The real winner, however, was the Sonoma County Fair whose officials attributed the year's record-breaking crowds directly to the publicity.

DRAGON RACE

Enter the Dragon was one of the first karate films and it was booked to open at the Grauman's Chinese Theater in Hollywood. To promote it, Warner Brothers's ace publicity stuntster Marty Weiser came up with the idea of staging a dragon race down Hollywood Boulevard between the chambers of commerce of the traditional rivals San Francisco and Los Angeles. San Francisco's dragon, brought out every Chinese New Year, was the most famous dragon in the world. Weiser called the San Francisco chamber of commerce, talked it into loaning him the dragon, and Warner Brothers paid to fly it down. They also paid to have twenty Chinese college students from San Francisco fly down and serve as the legs. Next, Weiser contacted the Los Angeles chamber of commerce and offered it the use of the dragon from the Warner Brothers movie *What's Up Doc?* He hired twenty Chinese college students from Los Angeles to be the legs of that dragon.

Weiser arranged for parade permits, and on the designated day, Hollywood Boulevard was roped off. The race came off even better than anyone had hoped. The two dragons started racing and at first the Los Angeles dragon was in the lead but then it stumbled and went up in smoke. Weiser confessed how that happened in an interview taped in 1988: "Actually I had one of those smoke bombs inside the dragon to make it look good, a yellow bomb, and when they stumbled all this yellow smoke went out and it was just great for the cameras. No one questioned the smoke—they just loved it, it was a great show." San Francisco was declared the winner, though Warner Brothers certainly didn't lose.

In a twist on the hundreds of running events held all over the country since jogging swept the nation in the seventies, the Wall Street Rat Race, first held in 1986, required participants to run in business suits and carry briefcases. The first race was so successful promoters have made it an annual event. The race is staged on April 15, its entry blanks resemble tax forms, and the starting gun sounds just after 7 P. M. to celebrate last-minute filing. Even the distance to run 4(01)K (or four kilometers) is a take-off on taxes, a 401K being an optional retirement plan. The race was hatched by public relations agency Ruder and Finn to draw attention to one of its clients, the South Street Seaport, an upscale shopping center located near Wall Street. Despite its convenient locale, the center was not well known among Wall Street denizens and the agency's job was to make it more visible. They had the race route begin and end at the shopping center, thereby ensuring mention of the South Street Seaport in every news story. In the first year, almost a thousand people entered the race. Finishers were served champagne and caviar; dropouts were served subpoenas. The coverage was phenomenal in both the national and local news.

The Wall Street Rat Race is held each April 15 in New York City; business suits and briefcases are required attire.

CLEANING UP THEIR ACT

"The Great Graffiti Cleaning Contest," held in a New York subway, was designed to spotlight the Mobil Foundation's Clean Team Summer Youth Employment Program. For many years, the Mobil Foundation underwrote a program in which disadvantaged youths were given jobs cleaning and beautifying parts of the city. Participants were paid for their work and also trained in various skills so that they could qualify for better jobs.

Jane Wesman, of Jane Wesman Public Relations, came up with the contest when Mobil hired her firm to devise an innovative way to bring attention to this program. She approached the casts of two hit Broadway musicals, *Big River* and *42nd Street*, and asked them to be part of the contest to increase its visibility. On the day of the contest, two teams, each composed of five youngsters and five cast members, competed to clean the walls of the 50th Street subway station. The team with the *42nd Street* cast members won by covering a twenty-yard course of tile in thirty-nine seconds.

The contest was such an enormous media success, that Wesman decided to stage a new contest the following year. This one was "The Great New York City Playground Painting Contest" to publicize another aspect of the program. Cast members from the same musicals appeared again in what was billed as a rematch. Both teams painted sets of seesaws as the judges timed the race. It ended in a tie, but in terms of publicity everyone was a winner.

The winning Clean Team

Contests for a record of some kind began to be popular in the mid-1950s after the *Guinness Book of World Records* began publication. Ever since the first U. S. edition came out in 1956, various charities, institutions, and businesses have attempted to set *Guinness*-verifiable records as a way of focusing atttention on themselves. Even if the effort fails to make the record, it does make the news.

Bakers at the 1977 Orleans County Fair in Knowlesville, New York, prepare a ten-ton apple pie in an attempt to break their own previously set *Guinness* world record.

Residents of Mantua, Ohio, attempt to set a record for the world's largest single serving of mashed potatoes at the town's 1980 potato festival. The Pillsbury Baking Company's role in the contest is clear.

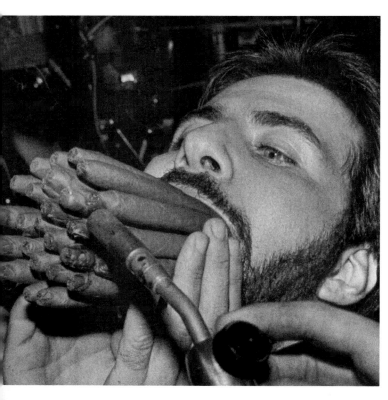

Keyboard player Mike Papa attempts to light twenty-seven cigars at once to promote his band, "Mouth." The once-popular cigar and pipe smoking marathons have fallen from favor in recent years.

A winning photo from a pie-eating contest sponsored by a Washington, D. C., boys club in 1955. Such contests are always popular.

This spaghetti-sucking contest was staged to publicize a New York City restaurant. Scantily dressed show-girls in competition practically guarantee maximum coverage from the media.

The Children's Aid Society sponsored an old-fashioned pigtail contest to bring attention to its charitable works. The longest pigtail won.

A 1975 attempt to build the world's largest ice cream sundae promoted a Wooster, Ohio, restaurant.

In honor of the dedication of the Hennepin Center for the Arts in downtown Minneapolis, Minnesota, 1,600 dancers tried to earn a spot in the *Guinness Book* for the most people tap dancing to a single piece of music at the same time.

Chapter 10

Legal Foolery

Lawbreaking, Lawmaking, and Censorship

> He who molds public sentiment goes deeper than he who enacts statutes or pronounces decisions. He makes statutes and decisions possible or impossible to be executed.
>
> Abraham Lincoln

Publicity seekers have long recognized that being banned, sued, arrested, or in any other way involved with the law is always legitimate news. P. T. Barnum demonstrated this knack for setting up legal embroilments when he had his bearded lady arrested for being an impostor. In the old days, people had fairly harmless or madcap schemes for getting arrested; nowadays the social protesters have co-opted the planned arrest as a deliberate tool of civil disobedience that is a guaranteed newsmaker. Unfortunately, there have been many instances of intentional lawbreaking as well by various publicity-seeking individuals from the lunatic fringe. However, in this chapter we'll walk the straight and narrow, focusing on the harmless and often ingenious schemes that involve the law.

A BREAKING STORY

From the beginning of his career, Salvador Dali exhibited a flair for publicity that rivaled his talent as a painter. By 1939 he had had a number of shows both in Europe and in New York, and was gaining some notoriety. Once he held a press conference in which he rather inexplicably brandished an eight-foot-long croissant. In another incident, he dressed a model in a mask of roses that covered her whole head and sent her to feed the pigeons in Trafalgar Square.

When asked to give a one-man show at the Julien Levy Gallery in New York, Dali felt it incumbent upon himself to stage a publicity stunt. It happened that the gallery had arranged for him to design some window displays for the Bonwit Teller department store on 5th Avenue. He created a grotesque tableau featuring, among other things, a bizarre mannequin floating in a bathtub filled with water. As soon as the windows were unveiled complaints to the store began pouring in and officials moved to close the windows off from public view.

Dali was so incensed at the attempted censorship that he entered one of the windows and pushed the bathtub through the glass. This move, he later maintained, had been unintentional—he had only meant to pour the water out. Whatever his intentions the results were instant headlines. As the *New York Times* put it, "Dali surged into the south window and carved his name on the police blotter." Another paper commented, "Through the window to fame." As a result of all the publicity, thousands of people came to the gallery show. In just two weeks, twenty-one of his works had been sold. Overnight, Dali became one of the richest artists in the world.

Attempted censorship will always improve the visibility of whatever is being attacked. One of Harry Reichenbach's most successful stunts occurred in 1913, early in his career, when he was hired by a small art gallery that sold prints. The gallery had stocked two thousand copies of a lithograph called *September Morn,* which pictured a nude girl standing in a quiet pool. Even at ten cents, nobody was buying it. Reichenbach took the picture and displayed it prominently in the window of the shop. Then he began telephoning Anthony Comstock, the head of the Anti-Vice Society. It took Comstock a while to respond, Reichenbach recalled. "I telephoned him several times, protesting against a large display of the picture which I myself had installed in the window of the art shop. Then I arranged for other people to protest and at last I visited him personally. 'This picture is an outrage!' I cried. 'It's undermining the morals of our city's youth!' I made him come with me and see for himself."

The offending art work, "September Morn"

Reichenbach had hired a group of young boys (at fifty cents each) to congregate in front of the window giggling and "making grimaces too sophisticated for their years."

At this sight the head of the Anti-Vice Society swung into action. He demanded that the picture be removed. When the gallery owner refused, the society took him to court. In the resulting hullabaloo, the obscure and rather mundane print became a famous work of art.

Reichenbach's stunt was copied in other cities by other exhibitors of the print to equally great success. The picture was banned first in New Orleans, where a gallery owner was arrested, and next in Chicago. Finally in May 1914, the First District Appellate Court of the United States ruled that the picture was not indecent—"although that may not be said of much of the exploiting to which it has been subjected," the court chastised. Eventually seven million copies of the print were sold at a dollar a piece. Reichenbach always regretted that he hadn't taken a percentage.

Broadway impresario Florence Ziegfield's career was built on a steady stream of publicity, and he always had a team of press agents working to promote his latest Broadway spectacular. But a stunt he hatched to promote his inamorata, Anna Held, was his own idea. He had brought Held from Europe and was giving her a big buildup to star her in upcoming productions. One day he found her bathing in a starchy white substance, a formula she had brought from Europe. It wasn't milk, but it gave him an idea. He arranged with a local dairy to begin delivering four hundred gallons of milk daily to the Savoy Hotel, where Held was staying. The original plan was that after several weeks Held would cancel the order and the dairy would sue her for nonpayment. This way all the world would learn that Anna Held took milk baths.

As the stunt progressed, however, Ziegfield decided to change his strategy. Instead, he sued the milkman—for delivering sour milk. This story was immediately picked up by all the newspapers. The *New York Times* reported that Held was suing the dairy for delivering sour milk and that the dairy was countersuing for nonpayment. Held's spokesman declared that "the matter will be settled out of court, as milk baths are too peculiar to be discussed in public." Shortly thereafter, however, Held, immersed in a tub of milk, held a press conference. She discussed with reporters all of the advantages of a milk bath for beauty.

For several days, the newspapers were full of news about Anna Held and her milk baths. Back at the hotel, Ziegfield and Held would giggle as they dumped milk down the drain. But the owner of the dairy, who had been in on the scheme, revealed the whole thing as a hoax. He was furious that his milk had been accused of being sour and complained that the situation was actually hurting his business. In the years that followed, journalists often cited the "milk bath" stunt as an example of the lengths to which a press agent would go for publicity.

DEMENTIA BRIDGEITIS

RKO studios brought contract bridge expert Ely Culbertson to Hollywood in the 1930s to make a series of short subjects. To publicize the series, the RKO publicists secretly paid a married woman to file for divorce, accusing her husband of "dementia bridgeitis."

The wife alleged that her husband "flew into a frenzy, kicked over a table and finally became so overwrought that he was placed under the care of a psychiatrist—because on one occasion she led hearts after his spade bid." At the time, the nation was caught up in a bridge-playing craze, and most people could be expected to agree that leading hearts after a spade bid might well justify attempted homicide.

To round out the stunt, the studio had the wife's attorney subpoena Culbertson as an expert witness. He testified to the fact that bridge could indeed lead to dementia. The story was front-page news, and the fact that the couple and the attorney were in the studio employ was never revealed.

THERE OUGHTA BE A LAW

Managing to get a law proposed or passed can be a great hook for publicity. For the Paramount movie *Seventeen*, a publicist named Leo Guild had a bill introduced into the New York legislature to lower the legal marrying age from eighteen to seventeen. The bill didn't pass, but the publicity mentioning *Seventeen* had its day.

The movie *Cold Turkey* was about the efforts of a small town to quit smoking. On its behalf, press agent Mac St. John arranged for the city council of Greenfield, Iowa, to declare smoking illegal inside the city limits. Not only did this generate publicity for *Cold Turkey*, but the town won many awards for public health awareness, boosting its own civic pride.

Russell Birdwell once approached the California legislature with an elaborate stunt for the movie, *The Young at Heart*. First he arranged for nine aging idols—former stars who had made millions but now were down and out—to be signed as extras in the film. Next Birdwell started circulating petitions to propose a law that would require the state to with-hold 10 percent of all stars' earnings for their old age. Birdwell called this law Career Insurance or The Manda-tory Film Savings Law. Although the idea never became law, it did become news. Birdwell was heavily criticized for capitalizing on people's misfor-tune, but he replied that promoting good causes was a PR man's "consti-tutional right."

Once Birdwell hired two interna-tionally known lawyers to handle a routine name change for one of his clients. K. T. Stevens was the daughter of a well-known movie director of the day, and Birdwell put it out that she was asking for a name change so she could avoid trading on her father's connections. Of course, the entire scenario was concocted to bring the fact of her parentage to the attention of casting directors, who had reason to want to be in good standing with her father. K. T. Stevens did capture some plum roles after the publicity game swung into gear, and her father apparently felt that his $20,000 was well spent.

The United Artists studio publicity department perpetrated one of the most inventive lawsuits on record. It had a restraining order issued by a Los Angeles judge forbidding charac-ter actor Louis Wolheim from having plastic surgery on his face. Wolheim, whose looks were distinguished by a large crooked nose that had been broken three times, played the heavy and "plug ugly" in many popular films of the 1920s.

A letter in the Lincoln Quarlberg Collection at the Motion Picture Academy library gives a rare look at the behind-the-scenes planning strat-egy of a great publicity stunt:

> Suppose, for instance, the UPI is given a tip that Wolheim is thinking about having his face remodeled—that he has been playing roles such as "The Hairy Ape" and "Capt. F." and only more recently the role in "Two Arabian Knights" that show his face in a way that makes people laugh. The tip further states that he has conferred with Dr. Balsin-ger in Los Angeles, and that it is rumored it will be one of the strangest facial operations—that of remaking a man's face that is so ugly. The tip might further state that it represents a $10,000 fee, etc. etc. etc.

Then suppose UPI releases a big story on the day wire which hits as many if not more papers than the AP, with four papers in New York, including the *World* and *Telegram*.

The story will be an exclusive interview with Wolheim by the UPI and will carry a byline over the wire. This is all set. If you recollect, I have on my staff a certain young chap named Quarlberg who formerly was the LA Bureau manager for the UP. The present Bureau Manager won his job there through Quarlberg, and is a very near and dear pal. In fact, this story will simply be written by Quarlberg and shot, as is, over the entire UP system.

The letter goes on to describe how, when Wolheim announced his intentions, the studio would respond by suing him, saying they had him under contract for the way he looked now and that he had no legal right to change.

The stunt came off exactly as planned. The *Los Angeles Times* reported the story for two weeks, beginning with Wolheims's proposed operation. "COURT MAY HALT SCHEME TO RE-ETCH ACTOR'S BUM RAP" was the headline for a story in which Universal Studio head John W. Considine was quoted as saying:

I am amazed at press accounts of a proposed facial operation upon Louis Wolheim, whom Howard Hughes of Caddo productions and I have under contract. For the information of those concerned, I want to announce that we have a legal contract with Mr. Wolheim in which he pledges his service to us as an actor. We engaged Mr. Wolheim because of his distinctive personality, and because his services are unique and distinctive. I do not intend to have his personality ruined by a so-called plastic operation. If necessary I will take legal action to prevent this operation, and I have served verbal notice to this effect on Mr. Wolheim.

Several days later the *Times* reported, in an article headlined "LOUIS CAN'T CHANGE HIS MAP:"

Louis Wolheim

All of the plaintiffs in their complaint assert that they have an equity in the nose which would be damaged irretrievably if Dr. Balsinger should operate. Wolheim, by sheer merit of his extraordinary olfactory equipment, it will be remembered, arose from the lowly status of professor of mathematics at Cornell Univ. to the glory of the films. With such a nose is he endowed that mothers are reputed to terrify squalling children into silence by mere mention of it . . . according to the complaint, after Wolheim had conquered Hollywood with his beak, and had become famous and valuable to his employers, he succumbed to the blandishments of life in the motion-picture capital and began to yearn for a new nose. He determined to cast aside the faithful, hard-working companion of his earlier struggles. . .

After hearing the arguments of both sides, the judge issued a temporary restraining order. Days later the parties were back in court for a judge to issue a permanent injunction. According to the *Los Angeles Times* report:

MR. WOLHEIM'S CARTILAGINOUS OLFACTORY PROTUBERANCE HAS TO STAY THAT WAY . . . LET BEAUTY LANGUISH AS IT MAY, JUDGE RULES: The plaintiffs contended Wolheim is under future contract and a Wolheim with a standard nose would be practically a dead loss. His nose has made him what he is today, the complaint recites: "The ugliest man on the stage." Wolheim's protest that a man's nose is particularly personal to himself and subject to his own discretion were of no avail against this argument. Judge Gates held that he had probably sold his nose in advance, just as it was, and that he would have to deliver it that way.

Wolheim continued to work with his ugly mug intact until his untimely death a few years later at age forty-nine. In what surely qualifies for the ultimate self-effacement (pun intended), he carried the secret of his complicity in the stunt with him to his grave, for his obituary, published in the *New York Times*, recalled, "In 1927 he arranged with a plastic surgeon to straighten his nose so that he might play romantic roles, as he declared he was tired of tough character parts, but the film executives obtained a restraining injunction."

MOTHER MAY I?

In a more contemporary mode, the left-wing national magazine *Mother Jones* managed to get a lot of publicity for itself when it generated a mock controversy about Ronald Reagan's endorsement of the decidedly right-wing publication *National Review*. During Reagan's presidency, the *National Review* ran an ad featuring Reagan's favorable comments about itself.

Mother Jones immediately wrote to Reagan asking for equal time. Reagan's office replied, saying that the *National Review* had not been authorized to use President Reagan's remarks. *Mother Jones* then pointed out that the unauthorized use of such statements for commercial purposes is against the law in most states and a violation of California Civil Code Section 3344 in particular. They wanted to know just what President Reagan planned to do about the *National Review*'s violation.

THE WHITE HOUSE
WASHINGTON

March 20, 1984

Dear Robin,

On behalf of President Reagan I would like to thank you for your letter. However, an endorsement for <u>Mother Jones</u> magazine will be impossible. President Reagan does not do endorsements for commercial publications. To set the record straight, President Reagan was invited to the opening reception for the Washington bureau of the <u>National Review</u> and accepted the invitation. His remarks at the reception were not intended as an endorsement of the magazine to be used for advertising. Again, thank you for your inquiry.

Sincerely,

Sue Mathis
Office of Media Relations and Planning

Robin Wolaner, Publisher
<u>Mother Jones</u>
1663 Mission Street
San Francisco, California 94103

MOTHER JONES
1663 MISSION STREET · SAN FRANCISCO, CA 94103
(415) 558-8881 · CABLE: MOTHER, SAN FRANCISCO, CA

March 27, 1984

Sue Mathis
Office of Media Relations and Planning
The White House
Washington, DC

Dear Ms. Mathis:

Thank you for your letter of March 20. We're shocked to learn that the <u>National Review</u> has made unauthorized use of statements President Reagan made at a party celebrating the <u>Review</u>'s new Washington office.

We are informed that the unauthorized use of such statements for commercial purposes is contrary to the law in most states and violates California Civil Code, Section 3344 in particular. Can you please let me know what action the president has taken or plans to take on this matter?

Sincerely,

Robin Wolaner
Publisher

P.S. We did not ask that the president "endorse" <u>Mother Jones</u> but, rather, that he "comment" upon us. Our offer to use any such comments in a subscription ad stands—provided, of course, that he authorize such use.

Chapter 11

Human Flies and Crash Peddlers
Daredevilry and Death-Defying Acts

After all there is nothing in life, paradoxically perhaps, which man so loves to see as his fellow man risking his life in an encounter with death.
Philadelphia North American,
reporting on Houdini stunt in 1905

When they hear "publicity stunt," many people think of and perhaps hope for death-defying, daredevil feats. Through the ages, performers of all kinds—acrobats, wire walkers, magicians—have risked life and limb to draw crowds and earn money. Examples of daredevils performing stunts for pay date back to antiquity.

True daredevils do what they do for the sheer sake of doing it. Philippe Petit gained international fame when he strung a wire between the towers of the World Trade Center and walked across it. Dan Goodwin climbed the face of the world's tallest building, the Sears Tower in Chicago, just because "it's there."

But many others—performers, professional stuntmen, and just plain attention seekers, have staged their risky stunts specifically to attract news coverage to a particular person, product, or event. People climb sides of buildings, jump off bridges, walk on high wires with no nets, use a variety of vehicles to jump over deep crevices or wide objects, go up in hot air balloons, jump out of airplanes, ride on the wings or dangle from the sides of airplanes, set themselves on fire, jump out of tall buildings onto big air bags—the variations are as endless as the clients they are promoting.

THE GREAT TRAIN CRASH

In the nineteenth century, the railroads were among the first large companies to hire press agents. As they opened new routes across the nation, they needed to publicize the various territories that had become accessible—to attract settlers and businesses along the vast frontier. At the time, runaway trains and train wrecks were a real and constant danger. In 1896, an official of the Missouri, Kansas and Texas Railroad (popularly known as the KATY) came up with the idea of staging a head-on collision as a publicity stunt to promote the railroad's new central Texas route.

The site selected for the crash was an area between Waco and Dallas, which then was perfectly desolate. There were no cars and no highways, just some dirt trails and the railroad tracks, the only connections between the two towns. A man appropriately named William Crush was put in charge of every aspect of the show. Not only was he responsible for planning and publicizing the crash, but it was also his job to create a small makeshift town for the thousands of people expected to gather at the barren site. This meant bringing in extra track, water, tents, and food and even building a small jail to house the inevitable troublemakers.

Two old locomotives were refurbished for the spectacle. Since this was the first time a collision had actually been staged no one was sure what would happen. One veteran railroad man predicted that the boilers in the steam engines would explode on impact, sending dangerous debris flying through the area, but this possibility was discounted by everyone else.

The stunt was announced with illustrated, four-color posters distributed throughout the KATY territory. Huge crowds arrived on the appointed day. According to some estimates, as many as fifty thousand people converged on the spot, all packed together on the hillsides that gently sloped up from the site. When the great moment finally approached, the two locomotives raced at each other from opposite points, attaining a speed of about sixty miles an hour. As they sped along to their final collision, they set off cherry bombs that had been fastened to the tracks, making frightening bursts. When the trains met, the explosion was more than the spectators had bargained for. Large pieces of the engines flew into the crowd and the people were too densely packed to run. Two people were killed and many more were injured—not at all the outcome one would hope for in a publicity stunt. To be sure, newspapers around the country covered the story, but other railroads were effectively dissuaded from ever trying to stage another collision. As for opening up the territory, today, close to one hundred years later, the site of the crash is still barren and unpopulated.

THE GREAT ESCAPER

Harry Houdini was one of the greatest self-promoters who ever lived. Throughout his career, he was constantly staging events especially for reporters, usually in a city where he would be appearing at a local theater.

One of his favorite stunts was to gather a crowd at a city's bridge, have himself manacled, and then dive into the water. He'd undo the locks underwater and after an uncomfortably long period emerge alive. Another crowd pleaser was to bind himself in a straight jacket and hang himself upside down from the top of a tall building. The crowd would cheer as he struggled to wriggle out of the jacket.

Houdini's prowess at self-promotion was such that he often was invited to speak to advertising clubs. "I get more advertising space without paying for it than anyone in the country," he bragged to one such gathering.

Harry Houdini wriggled out of a straightjacket hung from the Munsey Building in the nation's capital as thousands of people watched on April 19, 1916. Estimated at 50,000, the crowd was one of the biggest ever gathered in Washington up to that time.

In the early 1900s, "human flies" were climbing up the sheer fronts of buildings in record numbers. They climbed for personal publicity, a worthy cause, or for a few dollars. In 1923 a man named Harry Young was hired by the Hotel Martinique in New York City to climb its face. The management had agreed to pay him $40 but unfortunately he fell and died. New York City soon passed an ordinance making human flies illegal, but this didn't stop anyone who was determined. Even such unlikely climbers as the president of Abercrombie and Fitch once rappelled up the side of his building to publicize the company's excellent outdoor department.

Human fly Harry C. Gardner goes up the side of an unidentified building.

Leapers are another category of daredevils guaranteed to draw media attention. In 1982, Randy Miller, at age 22 the president of the Original New York Seltzer soft drink company, dove off the tenth story of a West Hollywood hotel into a giant air bag featuring his company's logo. He survived unscathed and the leap brought him and his soft drinks national publicity. The company continues to prosper.

An identical type of stunt was staged at the Vegas World Hotel in Las Vegas in 1984. The owner of the hotel paid a stunt man $1 million to plunge 326 feet from its roof into an air bag. At the time, the jump was a world record for the "high fall." It may also have been a record for the most money paid for a publicity stunt.

An aspiring playwright, hoping to attract a producer for his latest effort, jumped off the Brooklyn Bridge. Although he wore a wet suit and other padding to cushion his fall, he sustained critical injuries and was hospitalized for more than a month. Photographers and newsmen had been alerted to the jump in advance and were able to get some spectacular photographs of the leap. Police found a press release in the injured man's wet suit headlined "PLAYWRIGHT ON THE BRIDGE." Interviewed as he was being released from the hospital weeks later, the man confessed that he had not received one inquiry from a producer. He had no plans to repeat the stunt.

Other frustrated authors have been driven to desperate acts to gain attention for their writing. A Harcourt, Brace, Jovanovich author, angry at what he felt was a lack of promotion for his book, buzzed the publisher's Manhattan office building in a small plane. The stunt got him publicity all right—and an immediate arrest.

And in San Francisco, the author of *The Frisco Kid* climbed a tower of the Golden Gate Bridge. It is not known whether the sales climbed as a result.

**Frustrated writer
Dan Cameron
Rodill in his leap
for attention off
the Brooklyn
Bridge**

WILD PROTESTS

The daring act can be extremely effective as a gesture of protest. In Paris, for example, a man flew his private plane under the arch of Napolean's Arc de Triomphe to publicize the high cost of amateur aviation. The stunt, however, cost him his amateur license. In New York, a man climbed to the crown of the Statue of Liberty and threw off leaflets for a write-in campaign for mayor. In San Francisco, protesters from the environmental organization Greenpeace dangled a sign from the Golden Gate Bridge as a nuclear warship passed underneath. High winds made it impossible to unfurl the sign but at least no one fell in the attempt. The stunt held up traffic on both sides of the bridge, which probably didn't bring in any new converts to the cause. On other occasions, Greenpeace's challenges to whalers on the high seas have been extremely dangerous to their members but highly effective in bringing attention to the plight of endangered species in the seas.

A pilot's protest flight through the Arc de Triomphe in Paris

Exhibiting feats of physical strength is another way of gaining publicity. Fitness enthusiast Jack LaLanne made a tradition of performing difficult and daring physical feats every year on his birthday. LaLanne, who is credited with opening America's first modern health club in 1936, performed these stunts to attract attention to his clubs and health products. One year, wearing an air tank, he swam underwater across the San Francisco Bay. Another year he swam handcuffed from Alcatraz to Fisherman's Wharf. Twenty years later, upon turning sixty, he swam the same route with his wrists and ankles in shackles and pulling a one-thousand-pound boat. At age sixty-five, LaLanne flew to Lake Hakone in Japan and swam one mile, while towing sixty-five boats containing 6,500 pounds of wood pulp. (The wood pulp was provided by the Louisiana Pacific Forest Products Company in exchange for publicity). At age seventy, he swam one mile in the Long Beach California harbor towing seventy boats with seventy people aboard. Each year his efforts have brought him national coverage; they have been perfect gimmicks for keeping his name before the public indefinitely.

Jack LaLanne pulled ten boats filled with seventy-seven people a distance of one mile in less than an hour. This was in celebration of his sixty-sixth birthday in 1986.

Stunt flying for publicity purposes reached its height during the **twenties. Other variations included playing golf on the wings** **and airbound flagpole sitting.**

Epilogue

The World's Greatest Publicity Stunt Contest

*T*housands of publicity stunts went unreported in this book owing to space limitations. In fact, certain entire industries got short shrift. Missing, for example, are behind-the-scenes tales from sports, arguably one of the most hype-filled industries of all.

Politics is another ripe arena that I left for another book. Except in the photo essay on baby kissing and hat wearing, I have barely touched on the shenanigans of political aspirants and officeholders. Nor have I given religious leaders their just acknowledgment. Many have hired press agents to get their names and activities in the public eye and have come up with especially effective strategies for same. Recall Oral Roberts threatening suicide from his tower unless he received a multimillion-dollar donation, and Jerry Falwell, dressed in a business suit, going down a water slide to reward parishioners for their pledges.

Whole categories of stunts have yet to be explored—for example, what I call the "commemorative" stunt. This involves petitioning a government official to create a public event or declare a day or week in honor of someone or something. Such declarations are generally written by a press agent and then adopted by the targeted public figure as the official statement. Cynics are convinced that several of our most treasured national holidays were originally put forward by press agents for the greeting card and florist industries.

Creating a nickname for a client is another popular category virtually untapped here. In the early days of Hollywood, starlets were given nicknames in order to stand out from the pack. Clara Bow got miles of coverage as the "It" girl, Ann Sheridan was the "Oomph" girl, and Jean Harlow went unnoticed until her press agent coined the term "platinum" blonde just for her. Sports stars, too, get nicknamed— "Magic," "Boomer," "Refrigerator," "Blood" . . . the variations are endless.

Another tried-and-true PR approach is to buy an expensive insurance policy. Horror movie producer William Castle once took out a policy that insured each viewer of *Macabre* for $1,000 against death by fright. That got more attention than the movie itself.

Many omissions resulted from my decisions, but there are countless stunts, I'm sure, that I've never heard or even dreamed of—enough, I suspect, to fill an entirely new book. To fill the gap, I hereby announce a contest for the best and the most original publicity stunts ever enacted. Enough good responses could generate a sequel, and the winners will be included in that entirely new book, tentatively titled *The Return of Publicity Stunt!*

To enter the contest, send a one-page cover letter describing the stunt, copies of news stories and photographs of the stunt, and your complete name, company name, address, and work phone number to

Candice Fuhrman
P.O. Box F
Forest Knolls, CA 94933

Do not send original clippings or photographs unless you can spare them, because all entries will be nonreturnable. And no phone calls, please.

If you have a new category that I haven't covered or an industry you'd like to hear more about, tell me about that too. All winners will be contacted for more information and the creator of the stunt will be fully credited.

BIBLIOGRAPHY

BOOKS

Abel, Alan. *The Confessions of a Hoaxer.* New York: The MacMillan Company, 1970.

Agee, Warren, Phillip Ault, and Edwin Emery. *Introduction to Mass Communications, 7th edition.* New York: Harper & Row, 1982.

Bernays, Edward L. *Biography of an Idea: Memoirs of a Public Relations Counsel.* New York: Simon and Schuster, 1965.

Bernays, Edward L. *Public Relations.* Norman: University of Oklahoma Press, 1952.

Blyskal, Jeff and Marie. *How the Public Relations Industry Writes the News.* New York: William Morrow and Company, Inc., 1985.

Boorstin, Daniel. *The Image, or What Happened to the American Dream.* New York: Atheneum, 1962.

Brandy, Leo. *The Frenzy of Renown: Fame and its History.* New York: Oxford University Press, 1986.

Cantor, Eddie and David Freedman. *Ziegfield the Great Glorifier.* New York: Alfred H. King, 1934.

Castle, William. *Step Right Up! I'm Going to Scare the Pants Off America.* New York: G. P. Putnam's Sons, 1976.

Cutlip, Scott/Alan H. Center/Glen M. Broom. *6th Edition Effective Public Relations.* Englewood Cliffs: Prentice-Hall, Inc., 1985.

Deitz, Howard. *Dancing in the Dark.* New York: Quadrangle, 1974.

Fellows, Dexter. *This Way To The Big Show: The Life of Dexter Fellows.* New York: The Viking Press, 1936.

Goodman, Ezra. *The Fifty-Year Decline and Fall of Hollywood.* New York: Simon and Schuster, 1961.

Greene, Abel and Joe Laurie. *Show Biz: from Vaude to Video.* New York: Henry Holt and Company, 1951.

Hirsch, Abby with Dale Burg. *The Great Carmen Miranda Lookalike Contest.* New York: St. Martin's Press, 1974.

Kelley, Kitty. *His Way: The Unauthorized Biography of Frank Sinatra.* New York: Bantam, 1986.

Kominsky, Morris. *The Hoaxers: Plain Liars, Fancy Liars, and Damned Liars.* Boston: Little, Brown, 1986.

MacDougall, Curtis. *Hoaxes.* New York: The MacMillan Company, 1940.

Mackay, Charles. *Extraordinary Popular Delusions and the Madness of Crowds.* Boston: L. C. Page, 1956.

Maney, Richard. *Fanfare: The Confessions of a Press Agent.* New York: Harper & Bros., 1957.

Mayer, Arthur. *Merely Collossal: The Story of the Movies from the Long Chase to the Chaise Lounge.* New York: Simon and Schuster, 1953.

Mott, Frank Luther. *American Journalism.* New York: The MacMillan Company, 1949.

Orlando, Guido as told to Sam Merwin. *Confessions of a Scoundrel.* Philadelphia: The John C. Winston Company, 1954.

Reichenbach, Harry with David Freedman. *Phantom Fame.* New York: Simon and Schuster, 1931.

Re/Search editors. *Pranks!* San Francisco: Re/Search Publications, 1987.

Rogers, Henry. *Walking the Tightrope: The Private Confessions of a Public Relations Man.* New York: William Morrow and Company, Inc., 1980.

Schickel, Richard. *Intimate Strangers: The Culture of Celebrity.* Garden City: Doubleday, 1985.

Secrest, Meryle. *Salvador Dali.* New York: Dutton, 1986.

Silverstein, Herma and Carolyn Arnold. *Hoaxes That Made Headlines.* New York: J. Messner, 1986.

Subtle, Susan, Ruth Reichl, and Ken Dollar. *The Contest Book.* New York: Harmony Books, 1979.

Swanberg, W. A. *Citizen Hearst, A Biography of William Randolph Hearst.* New York: Charles Scribners Sons, 1961.

Washburn, Charles. *Press Agentry.* New York: National Library Press, 1937.

Wheeler, Michael. *Lies, Damned Lies, and Statistics: The Manipulation of Public Opinion in America.* New York: Liveright, 1976.

PERIODICALS

Abel, Alan (regarding):
"Alan Abel, Satirist: Created Campaign to Clothe Animals." *New York Times,* January 1980, obituary; "Dubious Achievement Award." *Esquire,* January 1968, p. 52; *Los Angeles Times,* February 6, 1980; "Obituary Disclosed as Hoax." *New York Times,* January 4, 1980.

"Actress Calls Fainting on 'Donahue' a Hoax." *The New York Times,* February 2, 1985, p. 42.

"Alleged Discoveries." *The Evening Post,* August 28, 1835 (editorial).

"Art Changed, Dali Goes on a Rampage in Store, Crashes Through Window into Arms of the Law." *New York Times,* March 17, 1931.

"Aw Gratin! Couch Potatoes Say Their Image Has Taken a Mashing at a California Couty Fair." *People,* August 8, 1988, pp. 46-47.

Bern, Henry. "Ivory Soap Sculpture Since 1925." *Procter & Gamble files,* January 1959; "Letter to A. H. Perrin." *Procter & Gamble files,* April 30, 1959.

Birdwell, Russell (regarding):
Article on Prisoner of Zenda stunt. *Time,* September 13, 1937, p. 32; *Box Office,* April 27, 1941; "He Can Make Anybody Famous for the Right Fee." *Cosmopolitan,* August 1961, p. 36; *Motion Picture Herald,* July 26, 1941; *Newsweek,* February 20, 1939, p. 40; *Newsweek,* November 29, 1943, p. 68; "Profile," *The New Yorker,* August 19, 26, and September 9, 1944; Ross, George. "So This is Broadway" (on Zenda stunt). *New York Times,* August 29, 1937; Typed memoirs. *Academy of Motion Pictures Arts and Sciences files. Variety,* October 31, 1938, November 2, 1938.

Bly, Nellie (regarding):
Articles on her trip around the world. *New York World,* November 14, 1889 through January 26, 1890.

Brand, Irving. "Stamp of the Press Agent Is Lasting." *Editor & Publisher,* June 12, 1920.

Broeske, Pat. *Los Angeles Times,* February 28, 1988, p. 4.

Castle, William (regarding):
Champlin, Charles. "Castle Operates Chilling Business." *Los Angeles Times,* August 30, 1965; Kobler, John. "Master of Movie Horror." *Saturday Evening Post,* March 19, 1960; Murphey, Mary. "Hawking Horror Films the P. T. Barnum Way." *Los Angeles Times,* November 6, 1973; "Only the real Thing Will Do for Director William Castle." *Box Office,* April 28, 1975; "William Castle 'Proves' Europeans Go for U. S. Exploitation Methods." *Box Office,* September 11, 1961.

Corkery, P. J. "For Immediate Release." *Harper's,* March 1982. p. 12.

Culbertson, Eli. *Los Angeles Times,* February 3, 1933.

Daley, Robert. "What Do They Do in Public Relations?" *Cosmopolitan,* December 1971, p. 150.

"Dali Show Opens at Levy Gallery." *New York Times,* March 21, 1939.

"Falwell Hits the Skids." *Time,* September 21, 1987, p. 33.

Frank, Allan Dodds and Lisa Gubernick. "Beyond Ballyhoo." *Forbes,* September 23, 1985, pp. 136-140.

Frank, Stanley. "Hollywood's Ballyhoo Boys." *Saturday Evening Post,* December 11, 1948, p. 34.

"Great Astronomical Discoveries." *The New York Sun,* August 25, 26, 27, 28, 29, 31, 1835.

"Herschel's Great Discoveries." *The New York Sun,* September 1, 1835.

"How the Press Agent Puts it Over Papers." *Editor & Publisher,* April 7, 1917.

Jaroslovsky, Rich. "She's No Doris Day, But for a Poodle She Sure Can Sing." *The Wall Street Journal,* September 8, 1975, p. 1.

Kalter, Joan Marie. "News That Isn't, (Really.)" *TV Guide,* September 22, 1984.

"The Man in the Moon." *The Evening Post,* September 1, 1835.

"Man Hatches Egg." *Life,* July 22, 1946.

Maney, Richard (regarding):
Article. *American Magazine,* October 1940, pp. 42-44; Article. *Time,* January 8, 1940, pp. 44-45; Profile. *The New Yorker,* October 11, 1941, pp. 27-32.

"More News from the Moon." *The Evening Post,* August 31, 1835.

"Moon Hoax Stories Built Circulation." *Editor & Publisher,* September 1959.

New York libel law. *New York Jurisprudence,* Vol. 42, Newspapers, sec. 3, p. 330.

Old John (regarding):
Articles. *New York Times,* April 9, 10, 11, 12, 14, 1922; "Old John Elephant Off on His Long Hike." *New York Evening Post,* April 10, 1922; "Old John, Star Trick Elephant 40 Years Ago, on 53 Mile Hike to Home of American Circus." *The World,* April 10, 1922.

"Puffs Should Be Excluded: Evil of Free Puffs for Advertisers." *Editor & Publisher,* September 21, 1901.

"The Press Agent." *Editor & Publisher,* May 17, 1902.

"Press Agents Liars?" *Editor & Publisher,* October 19, 1907.

"Publicity Microbe." *Editor & Publisher,* April 3, 1909.

Reichenbach, Harry (regarding):
Articles on *Virgin of Stamboul* stunt. *New York Times,* March 8, 10, 11, 28, 1920; *New York Times,* May 24, 25, July 28, 29, 31, 1920; June 8, 1924; July 4, 1931.

Smith, Pete (regarding):
Articles on flying lion stunt. *New York Times,* September 17, 18, 19, 20, 21, 1927; Editorial on flying lion stunt. *New York Times, September 23, 1927;* Goldstone, Richard. "The Cub that Roared." *New York Times,* January 1, 1928; Sellers, Al. "Pete Smith—Perfect Subject." *Hollywood Lowdown,* Holiday Number.

Spangler, Douglas. "Debunking Public Relations Myths." *USA Today,* January 1985, pp. 64-65.

"Stuart Little, 69, Publicity Agent." *New York Times,* May 29, 1968.

"Stranger Than Fiction." *Newsweek,* August 18, 1969, pp. 90-91.

Taylor, Robert Lewis. "Fiendish" (Profile of Roland Butler). *The New Yorker,* April 18, 25, 1953.

"They Thrive on Notoriety." *Editor & Publisher,* November 2, 1901.

"Uses Milk in Baths." *New York Times.* September 27, 1896.

"War Against Press Agents." *Editor & Publisher,* August 14, 1909.

Wolheim, Louis (regarding):
"Actor Breathes Easier Now." *Los Angeles Times,* October 31, 1927; "Court May Halt Scheme to Re-Etch Actor's 'Bum Pan.'" *Los Angeles Times,* October 28, 1927; "It's the Cast Nose of Summer." *Los Angeles Times,* November 9, 1927; "Louis Can't Change his Map." *Los Angeles Times,* October 30, 1927; Quarlberg, Lincoln. Letter. *Academy of Motion Pictures Arts and Sciences, Lincoln Quarlberg Collection;* "Wolheim to Have Face Remodeled." *Los Angeles Times,* October 27, 1927.